For Kendra

Thank you for your unwavering support

Empower Your Mind For Success, A Hypnotic Guide

How to Rewire Your Thinking for Massive Success

David R. Wright MA, LPC, CHt
www.motorcityhypnotist.com

Empower Your Mind For Success, A Hypnotic Guide

How to Rewire Your Thinking for Massive Success

By David R. Wright

First Printing: July 2021

ISBN 13: 978-1-7372072-0-7

David R. Wright MA, LPC, CHt

9333 Telegraph Rd, Suite 200

Taylor, MI 48180

313-452-0305

www.motorcityhypnotist.com

David R. Wright MA, LPC, CHt

Motor City Hypnotist, Inc.

9333 Telegraph Rd, Suite 200

Taylor, MI 48180

313-452-0305

www.motorcityhypnotist.com

David R. Wright is available to speak at your business or conference event on a variety of topics or to perform a comedy hypnosis stage show. Call (313) 452-0305 for booking information.

Why Read This Book?

Change your thinking, change your life.

What keeps you from experiencing success? Is it money? Time? Effort? Skill?

None of the above. The number one reason is your faulty belief system. Your embedded beliefs lead to all outcomes whether positive or negative. There is no simpler way to make permanent changes to your thinking that will lead to future success than hypnosis. Hypnosis has been around in one form or another for thousands of years and has been scientifically proven to be effective.

In this book, I'm going to break down all the reasons you fail and what you must do to succeed. It all starts with your thinking.

In this book you will learn:

- Why this time will be different for you

- What your purpose is. You will define what drives you and why you will finally experience success

- How to implement proven strategies including motivation, scheduling and address your belief system and how to avoid procrastination

- A full breakdown of what hypnosis is and why it is the most powerful tool to change your thinking

- I will walk you through how to enter a hypnotic trance and suggestions you can tell yourself that will forever change your life

This time, it WILL be different!

David R. Wright, MA, LPC, CHt, is a Licensed Professional Counselor and a Certified Hypnotherapist. He has been practicing clinically for almost 30 years. He currently hosts the Motor City Hypnotist Podcast and performs comedy hypnosis stages shows as the Motor City Hypnotist. He has hypnotized thousands of people from all over the United States.

Written by a Leading Expert with 30 Years Experience

David **R. Wright** is a Licensed Professional Counselor and a Certified Hypnotherapist. He is expert in helping people create lasting success. He performs hypnosis stage shows as the Motor City Hypnotist and has hypnotized thousands of people from all over the United States. Mr. Wright has been practicing clinically for almost thirty years and is currently the owner and clinical director of an outpatient mental health and hypnosis clinic located just south of Detroit. David also hosts the Motor City Hypnotist Podcast available now on all podcast providers.

Do you want David R. Wright to be the motivational speaker at your next event? Call (313) 452-0305 or visit www.motorcityhypnotist.com

Table of Contents

Introduction

S uccess is like a game. Everyone around you is trying to reach "the top," and there are times when you fall back a few spaces and end up having to work even harder to reach your goals.

If you believe that life is a game, you will most likely think that everything is determined by chance. However, success is not about rolling a pair of dice and expecting results in your favor. To succeed, you need positivity, motivation, and focus. These are the essential ingredients for success. But successful people take many more steps to reach that level.

While most people may refer to self-help books, motivational speakers, and spiritual leaders to find real success, I bring you a new and unique approach to help you find your path of success—*hypnosis*.

You may be skeptical about how hypnosis can help you achieve success but hang in there, and I will reveal a world of possibilities through hypnosis. With hypnosis, you can dig deeper into your subconscious and see what holds you back from achieving success.

People have been trying to understand hypnosis for more than 200 years now, and science has yet to explain what hypnosis really is. This piece of the puzzle is a small portion of a much bigger puzzle. However, mental health professionals understand the characteristics of hypnosis and are aware of how it works. It is a state of trance characterized by extreme suggestibility, relaxation, and heightened imagination. Hypnosis is not like sleep because, in this state, the subject is alert at all times. In fact, someone experiencing hypnosis is in a heightened state of awareness. Hypnosis is sometimes compared to daydreaming or to the feeling of "losing yourself" in a book or a movie.

Under the influence of hypnosis, you are fully conscious, yet you tune out all the stimuli around you except what the hypnotist/hypnotherapist is saying. You focus on the subject at hand so much that you exclude any other thoughts.

In the trance of a daydream or a movie, you begin to believe in an imaginary world that seems real to you, to the point that it fully engages your emotions. Fictional events can lead you to experience fear, sadness, or happiness. For me, I shed tears every time I watch *The Green Mile*. I am emotionally invested in the story. Some researchers even categorize these trances as different forms of self-hypnosis.

Hypnosis helps you get over your fears and allows you to focus on your goals. This becomes possible when your thought processes are changed, which ultimately leads to changes in behaviors. Hypnosis can be used for people who are trying hard to achieve personal and professional success.

Many famous people have turned to hypnosis for self-improvement. Huge names include Tiger Woods, Reese Witherspoon, and Julia Roberts, who have all used hypnosis to overcome their insecurities, making them more focused and in control of their goals.

My name is David R. Wright, and I am a Licensed Therapist and a Certified Hypnotist/Hypnotherapist. I use hypnosis daily in my office to help people overcome embedded subconscious habits. With the idea of motivating you to achieve success, I wrote this book to help you reprogram your mind so that you can achieve the success you are looking for in every area of your life.

If you take a closer look at successful people, you will find that they have common traits such as aspiration, drive, willingness to learn, patience, and discipline. You might think to yourself that you have never had the drive or motivation to do something. Or you may even believe that you lack the discipline or patience required to achieve success.

Here is the good news. You can develop all these

traits by simply changing your thinking. This is my purpose for writing this book. It may sound cliché, but it is a fact. Your thoughts drive your behaviors, good or bad.

I have been practicing clinically for twenty-nine years. I started my career even before I was out of high school. I began volunteering at a summer camp for teenagers for seven consecutive summers while in high school and college. I worked as a counselor to teens that attended the camp, and this experience led me to my calling in life.

During this time, I attended college and received a bachelor's degree in psychology. I went on to graduate school and obtained a master's degree in counseling. As I embarked on my journey as a therapist, I used different techniques such as relaxation, guided imagery, meditation, and mindfulness training. I then realized that I was using all the methods that make up hypnosis.

This led me to become a certified hypnotist/hypnotherapist, and I began using hypnosis with my clients. I used it to help my clients with quitting smoking, weight loss, anxiety reduction, and many more issues. To this day, I continue to use hypnosis with my clients so that they can make permanent changes to their thoughts, which results in changes in their behavior.

I have been thinking about this book for some time and, finally, I put pen to paper (and fingers to keyboard) and made it a reality. My motivation for writing this book is to reach a broader audience of people who want to make changes in their lives and achieve the success they have wanted for so long.

It has been my long-life dream to write a book. Therefore, my motives are not totally altruistic. I believe that by achieving my dream, I can help others achieve theirs too.

By the end of this book, I want you to make permanent changes in your thinking, manifesting changes in behavior and results. This will ultimately lead you to achieve levels of success that you may have only dreamed about. And by success, I mean in all areas. That includes your physical success, mental success, emotional stability, success in your career, and financial independence.

I want you to understand the beliefs and the ideas I explain in this book. I want you to know that it is possible to achieve your goals. It is all a matter of the mind. If you cannot believe you can achieve it, your belief will come true, and you will fail.

As this book progresses, I will show you how to remove the current limiting beliefs you have and to believe in yourself with a new approach. There are no limitations to belief. It is all within you. All you need to do is replace your old thoughts with new ones. I will help you experience the new truths, and eventually, it will become a part of you and your life.

I will help you change the old habits into new ones. These new habits will lead you to achieve your goals. Through this book, I will teach you to embrace and express the feelings inside you. And with those feelings, you can create your new vision. I will teach you how to overcome your fears.

Furthermore, this book will teach you about your subconscious mind and how you can access it. The subconscious mind has a lot of power. I will help you access that power and utilize it positively. Last but not least, this book will help you reprogram that subconscious mind through hypnosis.

I hope with all my heart that this book will help you achieve everything that you have dreamed of.

Remember. It is all in your mind!

Chapter 1
This Time Will Be Different

I just built a time machine.

Well, not really. But wouldn't that be cool? A time machine would allow you to go back and do things right. You could correct mistakes you have made, make different decisions, and transform the trajectory of your life. Some of my favorite books, movies, and television shows have to do with time travel. Some of my most recent favorites include the novel *11/22/63*. This Stephen King book (and now television series) tells the story of a man who goes back to 1963 to stop the assassination of JFK. Another of my favorites is the classic novel by H.G. Wells, *The Time Machine*. I was terrified by the Morlocks the first time I read that book. It is fascinating to imagine being able to go back or forward and change what has happened in the past or see what the future may bring.

Speaking of movies, excuse me while I geek out for a moment. In the film *Star Trek Generations*, Captain Kirk and Captain Picard are caught up in an energy field that allows them to go back to any time in the past or future. Kirk states, "I can start all over again—do things right from day one." Ah, if only science fiction were real, and we could start over from day one. Alas, that is not the case. You are where you are, right now in this moment of your life. You can only change what is in front of you, not behind. And therein lies the challenge for most of us. We are often victims of our past. Our experiences and failures have written a script. This script plays out in our subconscious minds repeatedly.

I loved baseball when I was a kid and grew up watching it with my dad, eventually playing little league. To say I was terrible is an understatement. I could not hit well and was average at best, defensively. Even now, I can recall my mindset at the time. I would be anxious and nervous before every game because my assumption was the same every game. My assumption was I was going to strike out often and that I would miss any ball that was hit to me in the field. I distinctly remember standing in the right field (where the awful players usually end up) and saying over and over to myself, *Please don't hit it to me. Please don't hit it to me.*

Fast forward to high school. I still loved the game

and persisted. There was a difference, though. I stopped playing the old script and focused on a new one. The new script excluded my past failures and focused on what I could do in the present. While I never came close to hitting .300 (an excellent average in baseball), I improved and averaged around .240. I also improved dramatically in my defense and *wanted* the ball to be hit to me. I earned my varsity letter during my sophomore year.

I flipped the script and wrote a new one. I was vastly improved and really enjoyed playing the game I loved.

Speaking of baseball, let's play a game. Don't worry. You won't need a bat or a ball. You will just need something to drink. Water is fine unless you may be in the mood for something more robust.

You are probably familiar with the drinking game Never Have I Ever. The rules of the game are simple. Someone makes a statement. For example, "Never have I ever punched someone in the face." I know. That's not a very nice thing to talk about, let alone do. If you have done the thing mentioned, the typical response is the person takes a drink, which tells everyone else playing that you have indeed channeled your inner Chuck Norris and threw your best haymaker. No, I don't condone violence in any form, whether it be a molly wop, fist kiss, or a knuckle sandwich. Regardless, the game goes on with each person taking turns, attempting to bring out the shocking truths from everyone's past.

If you were to google Never Have I Ever, you will find a myriad of posts and questions specifically for this game. Many of them are of the very juicy and embarrassing variety. One of my favorites I found while doing research is "Never Have I Ever really liked a song by Justin Bieber." [Raises glass and drinks.] Damn! Guilty as charged. I'm sure I'm not the only one who has an embarrassing Spotify playlist.

Let's play.

- Never Have I Ever doubted my own abilities.

- Never Have I Ever avoided starting something because I felt unqualified to do it.

- Never Have I Ever purchased an online course or product, thinking that I would follow through because of the financial investment, and didn't.

- Never Have I Ever dreamed about doing something and never taken action to make it happen.

- Never Have I Ever been told by other people that I have abilities and skills and internally scoffed at their statement.

- Never Have I Ever thought about making money doing something I love without pursuing that thought.

- Never Have I Ever viewed myself as inferior to others or lacking the confidence to start something new.

- Never Have I Ever experienced imposter syndrome. Imposter syndrome is defined as doubting your abilities and feeling like a fraud.

- Never Have I Ever worked on a project or task and said to myself, *This time will be different*, and it ended exactly as it always has.

Wow. That game wasn't nearly as fun as I thought it would be. My inner self is reeling, feeling like it has been beaten with a bag of nickels. Maybe you are feeling the same thing. Don't worry, my friend. This is the tough part. Cliché alert. Acknowledging your negative thoughts and feelings is the first step towards making change. My therapist's brain took over there for a moment.

Many famous people struggle with self-doubt and feelings of inadequacy. John Steinbeck stated the following when he was working on his Pulitzer Prize-winning novel *The Grapes of Wrath*, "I am assailed by my own ignorance and inability . . . Sometimes, I seem to do a good little piece of work, but when it is done, it slides into mediocrity." Emma Watson, the star of the *Harry Potter* films, among others, has admitted in many interviews that her low self-esteem made her extremely uncomfortable when pictures were taken of her. David Bowie stated in an interview, "I was driven to get through life very quickly. I really felt so utterly inadequate. I thought the work was the only thing of value."

It may come as a surprise to you, but we have all been there. We have all had or have self-doubts and a lack of confidence. We will always have areas that we feel ill-equipped to handle. God forbid someone asks me to perform brain surgery tomorrow. An extreme example, to be sure, but there are many more things that I would not be able to do successfully compared to the things I am competent in. The key is identifying where our strengths lie and to expand and perfect those areas.

I dabble in investments. It is something that has always fascinated me, and I've watched so many YouTube videos, you would think I was a teenage gamer. John Templeton wrote a famous book about investing called *16 Rules for Investment Success.* In the book, he states, "The investor who says, 'This time is different,' when in fact it's virtually a repeat of an earlier situation, has uttered among the four most costly words in the annals of investing."

Even though he is referring to financial loss, this statement can be applied to our own flawed thinking. Our downfall is continuing to believe that things will be different without changing anything. It is like a ship drifting along on the ocean, swept here and there by the winds and the captain just hoping things will work out. It is not a very efficient approach, matey.

Author Martin Meadows wrote a book called *"This Time Will Be Different: A Short Book on Making Permanent Changes*. He states in this book, "Nothing will change in your life if you don't feel that you have to do something about your situation." He is bringing to light the cycle that we have all experienced. We continue to do the same things and hope for different results. Until you change the underlying thinking, which will lead to changes in behaviors, it will always be "just like last time."

Why do you do the same things over and over again when it does not lead to success? There are many answers to this. The most basic and simple answer is that you don't know any other way. You have learned to function based on your experiences and history. Author Tim Ferriss states, "The best results in life are often held back by false constructs and untested assumptions." We are going to address the idea of false constructs later in this book.

You might be asking yourself, "how long will it take

to be different?" That is a very tricky question. Long answer short, it depends. Are you ready for change? Is change something you really want to experience? Are there fears that hold you back from making significant changes in your life? Author E. James Rohm states, "Success is neither magical nor mysterious. Success is the natural consequence of consistently applying basic fundamentals." I am going to teach you the basic fundamentals that can have drastic positive effects on the way you think, feel and act.

Most people are not living the life they want. Most people are mired in mediocrity. You may be one of those people. Maybe you know someone who fits in this category. We have been trained in mediocrity since our childhoods. Mom and dad may have been caring and supportive. They probably also fed you these encouraging statements: "We're proud of you no matter what"; "You're so smart"; "You're so handsome/pretty." I am not saying these are not good statements. Of course, we want to encourage children and bolster their self-esteem. However, these statements are not necessarily true. In fact, in most cases, they are probably blatantly false.

If you have ever taken a statistics class (cue the groans), you probably know what a bell curve is. A bell curve charts the normal distribution of data in a population. If you fall right in the middle of the bell curve, you are average (we will skip the median/mode aspects of the bell curve for now). This means that most of us are average in most things as the majority of the population falls in the middle of the bell curve. We have specific strengths and weaknesses. Maybe you excel in music, writing, or juggling on a unicycle. But overall, we are average. That is just how life is. To become truly great at something, you have to put in the time, effort, and practice to be excellent. This is the difference between success and failure.

You are reading this book because you are ready to change. The cycle of failure is simply something from your past. This time can and will be different because you are choosing to make it different. Simply just committing to something will have tremendous impact and influence on all your future experiences. Decide, right now, this time *will* be different. Say it out loud. Write it down. Now that your decision to change is made, I will guide you through the steps to ensure that this time will indeed be different.

Chapter 2
Purpose Defines You

In this chapter, we will define your vision and lock in what your future successful self looks like. You will drill down deep and find out what you are passionate about. We want to know exactly what brings you joy and happiness. In the words of Agent Smith from the Matrix films, "Without purpose, we would not exist. It is purpose that created us. Purpose that connects us. Purpose that pulls us. That guides us. That drives us. It is purpose that defines us."

Let's talk about what most people are doing. Most people get up, go to work at a job that they hate, work eight, nine, or ten hours, come home, have dinner, spend some time with the family, maybe watch television, and rinse and repeat. Now, I am not necessarily saying this is a bad thing. If someone is genuinely passionate about their work and feels great doing it, this could be a good thing. Unfortunately, many are locked into a job because it pays well or has good benefits. Most people work to support themselves and their families, but they are not genuinely passionate about what they do. It does not give them a sense of purpose or actual happiness.

When I was working my way through college and graduate school, I had many jobs that I did not like. Many of the jobs I just plain hated. I worked in food service when I was in college, and I dreaded each and every shift. At the time, it was necessary to work that job as I was paying for school and earning some spending money. Much of that spending money was dropped into the dorm vending machines at 3:00 am while studying for an exam or writing a paper. During my time in graduate school, I worked the midnight shift at a group home for the developmentally disabled. While the work was admirable, I distinctly remember watching the clock, and the eight-hour shift felt like days. You have also likely experienced the dreaded time drag. Just like the old saying, a watched pot never boils, a watched clock moves sloooowly.

When I finally graduated with my master's degree in counseling, I began working a job that I enjoyed, and that gave me purpose. I am rewarded personally by helping other people feel better and resolve their issues. To put it in a different context, I am no longer working at a job. I am enjoying a career, and I have meaning and purpose.

Now imagine that you go to work each day. You feel a sense of purpose, a feeling of happiness and motivation because you LOVE what you do. And imagine being able to experience that feeling day after day. That may be owning your own successful business. Or perhaps it is designing your online course. Maybe it is writing your book. Whatever it is, it needs to be something you are passionate about, something that you care deeply about doing because it will give you a sense of purpose.

Let's go through these questions that will help you define your vision.

1. Identify things that you can do to help improve the lives of others.

2. Think back to an activity that made you forget about time (time flew by).

3. What things did you love to do as a kid?

4. What do people come to you for? Advice, technical assistance, help building something?

5. What would you be doing right now if you realized you only had a year to live?

6. If you were able to teach others, what would you teach them?

7. Name an activity that you would do for free (not being paid for).

8. What do other people thank you for?

Hopefully, these questions have helped you become aware of something that you would love to do. When I work with clients, I will sometimes ask them what they really enjoy doing. I had one client recently who told me, "I like to watch movies," and the client laughed and went on to say, "I know, that's a waste of time." I responded by asking the client if it is something they enjoy, how is it wasted time? I went on to explain that there are many people out there making a living by watching TV. There are tons of reaction channels on YouTube where people simply watch movies and TV shows and film their reactions.

We could just rely on our passions and interests, but often, your passions alone may not dictate whether you would be happy and fulfilled in a career or job. We must also examine the deeper levels of what your career would mean to you and if your abilities and skills will allow you to succeed in a specific career. I am passionate about sports. However, my abilities (or lack thereof) did not allow me to pursue a career as a professional athlete. It is crucial that you are honest with yourself and your skills to find something that you are passionate about *and* is within your abilities and skillset.

It is also important to note that you can learn to do something well. While it might not be within your skillset presently, it may be possible to increase your skillset depending on what you are aiming for. The most vital thing is that your goal is realistic and obtainable. We can go back for a moment and reinforce that your past failures do not have to dictate your future limitations. But you do have to be realistic and logical about your abilities.

What are some predictors of job satisfaction? A study by 80000hour.org was completed covering numerous psychology books, papers, and a Google Scholar search for relevant terms and job satisfaction literature in the OSHwiki (Occupational Safety and Health). The research resulted in the PERMA Theory created by the founder of positive psychology, Professor Seligman. The PERMA Theory summarizes the key ingredients of living a fulfilling life as follows:

- Positive Emotions – feeling happy day to day.

- Engagement – challenging, absorbing tasks.

- Meaning – having a purpose higher than yourself.

- Relationships – connecting with others.

- Achievement – being good at something.

Simply put, any career or job that meets all of the criteria shown should provide a level of meaning and satisfaction that, more likely than not, will be rewarding for you. Now it is time to combine the questions you answered to help define your vision and see if any of the answers meet all of the PERMA Theory ingredients.

"Deciding to focus on vision means determining the way you want your life to go. To create a life where you're thriving, not just surviving, you must focus on creating a compelling future. Pick anything – a goal, dream, or desire – that you want so much, you're going to find yourself compelled to make it happen. Don't be modest or shy about what you want to do with your life. Dream big: What legacy do you want to leave behind? How do you want people to remember you?" As Tony Robbins asks, "What would you have to accomplish to look back at your life and say, "I have no regrets?"

https://www.tonyrobbins.com/stories/unleash-the-power/focus-on-your-vision/)

If you have no vision, you have no why. You must define as clearly as possible what your why is because it is this why that is going to drive you to push through when things are difficult. It is your why that will keep you on track with your goals and desires. Your why defines how and why you do the things you do each and every day. Without a why, there is no purpose, no reward, no fulfillment.

Chapter 3
How to Guarantee Failure

This chapter is a bit tongue in cheek, but it will give you great insight into habits you may be struggling with right now. There are endless lists online that guarantee success. We are going to take a different route for this chapter. There is an infinite number of ways to succeed. But there are a limited number of ways to guarantee failure. The goal for you is to eliminate any of these habits from your life. Of course, to stop something, we must recognize that it exists. This will require you to be honest with yourself.

Many famously successful people have a long list of failures.

- **Stephen King**

  King's first novel, Carrie, was rejected thirty times before it was published. King threw the manuscript in the garbage. It was retrieved by his wife, who told him that he was onto something with that story.

- **Jim Carrey**

It is hard to believe Jim Carrey anything other than the zany, funny star we know him as today. However, he grew up in a low-income family with a father who struggled for work. His family was so poor that he had to drop out of high school at the age of fifteen to get a job as a janitor to financially help his family. He was booed off stage while performing his first standup comedy routine in Toronto. Later, he auditioned for *Saturday Night Live* and failed to land the part.

- **J. K. Rowling**

Everyone knows about *Harry Potter*, even if you are not a fan. J.K. Rowling lost her mother to multiple sclerosis (MS). She was teaching English in Portugal, was married, and had a child. Her marriage ended in divorce, and she moved to Edinburgh, Scotland. She viewed herself as a failure and suffered from bouts of depression, eventually signing up for government-assisted welfare.

These are just a few examples of phenomenally successful people who struggled with setbacks and failures. Their tenacity and refusal to quit enabled them to achieve their successes eventually. We will touch on motivation and commitment later in this book.

There are many books and articles out there that

explain why failure is essential and the important lessons we learn from our failures. I cannot argue the point and will address how we learn from failure in an upcoming chapter. However, I want to emphasize that we can learn from failure *before* it happens as well. Remember the time machine I referenced in the first chapter? Let's travel to the future and head off significant failures before they happen (and avoid the Morlocks). You can do that by eliminating these things that will doom your success.

Fail to plan for your future.

Failing to plan for your future will guarantee no direction and chaos in your life. Not planning is a sure-fire way to fail to accomplish your goals. Imagine waking up each day without any type of schedule or plan. You might get a couple of things done as you meander about the house in your underwear, looking for something decent on daytime television or the millions of streaming channels you subscribe to. Do you believe that successful people wait around for something good to happen without any type of plan? Benjamin Franklin stated, "If you fail to plan, you are planning to fail."

I had a brief fascination with architecture when I was in high school drafting class. While it did not lead to a career in architecture, it gave me insight into building and how things are constructed. As you are reading this book, you are probably in a house, apartment, or another living area. Would you feel safe in that area if you knew it was built without any planning? If workers had just shown up every day and winged it without planning, the structure would undoubtedly be flawed.

Planning gives us order and direction. So why do we fail to plan? The simple answer is entropy. Entropy is "the lack of order or predictability; gradual decline into disorder." This term is often used concerning thermodynamics; however, I am not a scientist, and I'm sure you probably do not want this book to read like a science textbook. Anyone who has had a teenager in their home is probably familiar with the last part of the definition, "gradual decline into disorder." I'm referring, of course, to your teenager's room. Left to run its course naturally, the disorder is the ultimate outcome.

Let me quote author James Clear who wrote this blog *Entropy: Why Life Always Seems to Get More Complicated.* "What is entropy? Here's a simple way to think about it: Imagine that you take a box of puzzle pieces and dump them out on a table. In theory, the pieces can fall perfectly into place and create a completed puzzle when you dump them out of the box. But in reality, that never happens. Why? Quite simply because the odds are overwhelmingly against it. Every piece would have to fall in just the right spot to create a completed puzzle. There is only one possible state where every piece is in order, but there are a nearly infinite number of states where the pieces are in disorder. Mathematically speaking, an orderly outcome is improbable to happen at random."

Let me stress that last sentence: "An orderly outcome is doubtful to happen at random." I have many clients that come into my office whose lives are in disarray. They are overwhelmed with responsibilities and feelings of being "buried." Why? Because they are living life randomly. They are just reacting to situations and not taking control to manage situations before they become problems. They are constantly "putting out fires" rather than practicing fire prevention. Planning is the key to your fire prevention.

Blame everyone else for everything wrong that happens in your life.

The dreaded blame game. Blame causes individuals to be unwilling to accept responsibility for their part in any issue or situation. Unfortunately, we are living in a society where blame is prevalent. Reality television is built upon conflict, arguments, and blame. Without the conflict and blame, the shows would not be nearly as successful as they are. Politics is filled with blame (politics has always been a hotbed of blame and derision).

When I was working during college at the university food service, I had one co-worker who was always late. And when I say always, I mean every shift. He would always have some type of excuse. His alarm didn't go off, he got held up in class, he was sick, or aliens had abducted him. He was eventually let go, but I always wondered what was going on with him. He would not take responsibility. I am hopeful that he finally figured out that he would not move forward and succeed in life unless he started taking responsibility for his actions.

Why do we blame others for our shortcomings or mistakes?

First, it is easier to blame other people or situations because we don't have to take responsibility, and there is no accountability. It is a hit to our ego to admit that we screwed up or that we are not perfect. It is much easier to force the focus onto something or someone else.

Second, it feeds our need for control. When we admit that we made a mistake or screwed up, we are revealing a weakness. I don't know anyone who likes to admit weaknesses because it diminishes your control over a given situation. On the plus side, if we recognize our shortcomings, we can address them and make positive changes.

Don't ever focus on your physical health and wellness.

You may know or may even be what we call a Type A personality. Characteristics of a Type A personality are competitive, impatient, domineering, and overly ambitious. While these traits are positive and Type A personalities are often successful, it is frequently at the expense of their own physical and mental health. Type A personalities suffer from stress-related health problems, hypertension, social isolation, and irritability. The website Verywellmind.com references an in-depth study performed more than forty years ago. The study showed that Type A personalities were at a seven-fold increased risk of developing coronary artery disease and that most of them experienced heightened anger and hostility.

Physical and mental wellness will allow you to maintain a greater quality of life without unnecessary fatigue or stress. This, of course, will have a massive impact on your overall health and quality of life.

Make goals that are general and have no timeframe.

It's great that you have plans. However, it is crucial that your goals meet specific criteria. You may have heard of the term S.M.A.R.T. goals. There are entire books written just about goal setting so that we won't get too deep into it here. However, it is vital that your goals are specific, measurable, attainable, realistic, and time-bound.

I had a goal to write a book. I have had this goal for years, and yet, it is just now a reality. Why? Because my goal was general, I had no time frame and was not time-bound. General goals are like dreams. You can sit and think about them all day long, but they will stay right where they are, dreams, unless they are bound by action.

If you have a goal, be sure it meets the S.M.A.R.T. criteria and visit the progress of that goal daily. You should also have your goals broken up into short-term and long-term goals. Keep a journal or post your goals where you will see them often to keep you on task and to remind you of what you are working towards.

Just do the same thing every day.

This one fits in with fail to plan; however, this is even more frustrating. There is a famous quote often incorrectly attributed to Albert Einstein: "The definition of insanity is doing the same thing over and over again and expecting different results." The quote was actually from a Narcotics Anonymous pamphlet published in 1981. The original quote states, "Insanity is repeating the same mistakes and expecting different results."

Let me reference another client's story. I was working with a forty-ish-year-old female. She felt stuck and told me she felt like she was in the movie *Groundhog Day*. Every day she would follow the exact same routine: Up at 6:00 am, get the kids ready for school, make coffee, pack lunches, drive the kids to school, go to work, take lunch from 1:00-1:30, leave work at 5:00, pick up the kids from after school program, drive home, make dinner, clean up, watch television for an hour and go to bed.

I suggested that she needed to change her routine, shake up the schedule. She was resistant at first, stating, "I don't have time" and "no one else will do it" (referring to picking up the kids). After some conversation, she committed to taking fifteen minutes from the hour she usually watched television and work out for those fifteen minutes. That small change made a massive difference in the way she felt and her feelings of being in a rut. That fifteen minutes eventually expanded to an hour. We then worked together to make arrangements for a close friend to pick up the kids., which gave her another hour to herself in the afternoon. Long story short, we did a pattern-interrupt (a term we often use in hypnosis) and changed her version of *Groundhog Day*.

She is now making time for herself and delegating what she can to focus on her own physical and mental health.

Always stay angry.

Human beings have emotions. That is part of what makes us the complicated beings we are. Anger is one of the most damaging and dangerous emotions, often leading to verbal and physical confrontations. Anger, in and of itself, is not the real issue. It is our response to the feeling of anger that gets us into trouble.

Practicing clinically for almost thirty years, I have seen countless clients with anger issues. Some types of euphemisms for angry people include hotheads and short-tempered. Types of anger you have likely heard about may include road rage, fuming, and blowing a gasket. While these can be humorous, there is nothing funny about someone losing their temper and lashing out.

Anger always comes from some other emotion. It does not exist in a vacuum. If a couple is arguing, one partner may become angry because they feel insulted or dismissed. A bar fight can break out because an individual feels slighted or disrespected. Your teenager may throw the video game controller across the room because he or she is frustrated.

When you are angry, you must identify the underlying emotion that is driving the anger. Sadness, embarrassment, and frustration can all lead to anger. There can also be physiological causes. Blood sugar levels, hunger, and pain can all cause feelings of anger. Anger will often cause a reduction in cognitive processing and the ability to correctly recognize external stimuli.

Identify the underlying emotion and express that emotion. If you are angry with your partner because he/she called you a name, try responding, "What you said really hurt my feelings." You must resist the urge to escalate and retaliate. This can be difficult for many people as it makes you vulnerable. With practice and recognition of the underlying emotion, you can de-escalate your anger and express yourself constructively.

Complain to others and yourself constantly.

Do you know someone who is a complainer? We all have that friend or family member who is constantly complaining and whining about everything. Maybe you are one. That's okay. We are going to change that by the time you are done with this book.

Can you imagine living with George Costanza day after day? George is one of those characters who constantly complains about everything and rarely does anything to improve his situation or surroundings.

Author Israelmore Ayivor states in his book *Daily Drive 365*, "Empty complaints are the sources of everyday failure, but not the problem being complained about. Problems are solvable, but not with complaints. A complainer is just an explainer of problems!"

The company Reputation Builder performed a study and found that customers who have a bad experience are twice to three times more likely to write an angry review than customers who had a great experience are to post a happy review. Researchers have found that human beings are much more likely to spend time and energy reviewing and dissecting bad experiences rather than good ones. Need proof? Just spend an hour or so on Facebook. Now, I know, social media is its own little world and not a total reflection of real life. People tend to be much more outspoken behind a keyboard than they would be face to face with another human being. Yelp has become a breeding ground for thousands of George Costanzas. A one-star restaurant review complained about an incident that occurred while visiting a restaurant that had more to do with the mobility issues of the individual and not to do with the restaurant, lashing out in anger at the restaurant owner.

Complainers are going to complain. The Harvard Business Review states research shows that chronic complaining has physiological effects. Through repetition of bad, sad, mad, and powerless feelings, the neurotransmitters in the brain can go through a neural "rewiring," which reinforces negative thought patterns. We are going to address this phenomenon in a later chapter. Repetition creates habit. Be aware of complaining and negative thinking.

Never do anything new or challenging.

Humans are creatures of habit. We like our routines and set schedules. We don't like being inconvenienced by new experiences or getting out of our comfort zones. A sure way to remain average is never to try anything new or challenging. If you never try something challenging, you are less likely to fail. That keeps you right where you are . . . the status quo.

One of my favorite movies of all time is *Dead Poets Society*. If you have not seen the movie, I highly recommend it (be ready for an emotional roller coaster). Without giving spoilers, the story focuses on a boarding school English teacher played by Robin Williams. He challenges the boys in the class to think for themselves and to make their lives extraordinary. With simple exercises like eating with their opposite hands or creating their way of walking, he encourages them to break out of their comfort zones and to experience things in a different way.

Break out of your daily habits. Do things differently. Researchers have found that whenever you do something that evokes an emotional response, or that is out of the ordinary, your mind recognizes that this is important; something is different. This happens during childhood when our brains are like sponges. Children take in so much information as they are constantly experiencing new things and their brains store that information. That is why we can recall a lot of information about experiences from childhood. Still, as we progress in adulthood, we have a more difficult time remembering experiences because most of our experiences are routine. Other than an occasional vacation or party, there is nothing remarkable for your brain to lock onto.

Believe in overnight success.

Sudden success is rare. Overnight success is even rarer. The belief that you start a successful business or make some earth-shattering difference overnight is misleading. There are those rare stories of people who have skyrocketed to success, fame, and fortune. However, that is like saying my neighbor won the lottery. I need to get my ticket right now. Immediate success is the exception to the rule. You're also probably not getting all of the details of these success stories.

In his book *On Writing*, world-famous author Stephen King states that he pinned every rejection letter he received to his wall on a nail. By the time he was fourteen, the nail in the wall would no longer support the weight of the rejection letters impaled upon it. He replaced the nail with a spike and went on writing.

Success comes with planning, effort, tenacity, and a vision of what you want to accomplish. You will be surprised and amazed at times when doors open that you didn't even know existed. A couple of years ago, I had issued a press release for a golf performance hypnosis recording. A couple of local news outlets picked it up, and I did an interview with one of the local television stations in Detroit. Within a week, I had two requests (one from *Hour Detroit Magazine*) wanting to talk to me about hypnosis and smoking cessation. They had seen the press release about golf and went in a different direction. Another door opened that I wasn't even targeting.

Give up whenever you meet resistance or difficulties.

A sure-fire way to fail is to give up when things become difficult. It's called resistance and is an inherent characteristic of change. I am one of those people who purchased a gym membership . . . numerous times. When I joined (on each occasion), I had high hopes and aspirations to get in shape. A couple of times, I even stayed with it for a time (at one stretch over the course of years). In the other instances, I ran into resistance. I was gung-ho and motivated for the first few months. Then resistance hit. It started becoming more difficult to fit into my schedule, or I ended up getting a cold and thought I would just take a week off. I took a couple of mornings off because I wanted an extra hour of sleep. Normal, everyday things dampened my motivation, and I quit.

Resistance can manifest in many ways: procrastination, making excuses, delaying, wasting time, perfectionism, self-sabotage, low motivation and mood, taking a break, or just plain giving up. Resistance is that wall that marathon runners will tell you hits them at about the eighteen-to-twenty-mile mark. This happens because glycogen levels run low, and the body signals the brain to shut down, leading to negative thinking. Many runners will tell you that the wall is a psychological barrier that they must break through.

While I have never run a full marathon myself, I was on the cross-country team in high school. Cross country runs are 3.1 miles. Admittedly, I would probably collapse if I tried running 3.1 miles right now. I distinctly remember those times during meets when I would be two to two-and-a-half miles into a race, and my mind would start yelling at me to STOP! Some mental techniques can be utilized to help get past the wall. You can recite a mantra, notice your surroundings, break it down into manageable chunks, keep in mind your ultimate vision. These strategies can work in a personal and professional setting as well. Know that resistance is part of success, and you will hit the proverbial wall. You must push through it to reach your ultimate goal.

Make excuses for everything.

We all make excuses from time to time to deal with our failures. We use this simple habit to rationalize why we didn't meet our goals or finish our objectives. Some of the most common excuses are: "I'm too old to start"; "I'm not talented enough"; "I'm not smart enough"; "I don't have time"; "I don't have the money"; "I don't have support"; "I lack motivation"; "I don't have the education"; "I'm not ready yet"; "I'm scared." Every one of these examples is an excuse, a reason that you tell yourself you cannot succeed. It gives you comfort because you are in a dead-end job, doing something you hate doing because accepting that these are excuses forces you to examine your lives and take responsibility for where you are at.

When one considers being too old as an excuse, I think of Dr. Seuss, who wrote *Cat in the Hat* when he was fifty-four years old. A personal example of my own is my father, who was a blue-collar worker his entire life working at a steel mill here in the Detroit area. When he was around fifty-five years old, he was laid off (along with all his other aged fifty-plus co-workers). While that would be illegal today, back in the early eighties, it happened. He went to school and became a registered nurse. He worked as a nurse in a Detroit area hospital and in-home care for over 15 years until he retired.

Another common excuse for not having the money brings to mind some of the most successful people in the world who rose from poverty to become successful. Oprah Winfrey, LeBron James, and Gordon Ramsey all came from impoverished families. While I understand that money can provide greater access and advantages, being poor does not disqualify you from success.

I can quickly go through all of the items mentioned above and debunk each and every excuse. When I work with clients in my office, I am often presented with excuses for why the client cannot change. Change is a choice. Staying the same is also a choice. It is one or the other. By doing nothing, you are choosing to stay precisely where you are. Make a choice to be where you want to be, no excuses.

Spend all of your free time online or watching television.

There is a lot to cover in the statement above. However, the theme remains constant—wasted time. I'm not saying that you should never watch television or spend time online. I happen to enjoy a few television series and am a big *Marvel* fan. However, I limit the times for these activities, and they don't take the place of essential things that I am working on (such as writing this book). I want you to do something. For a week, write down and account for every minute of every day. At the end of seven days, look back and see where most of your time went. If you find that most of that time was spent doing things that do not promote success, it is time to re-prioritize your time.

The internet is one of the biggest time-suckers there is. I have been there many, many times, allowing it to drain time. I typically get to work around 8:30 am each day. I start my day by reviewing my schedule, looking at emails, responding to anything that needs action, and then catching up on the news. Invariably, I end up popping onto social media. I'm not a huge fan of Facebook, but it is a necessary evil because I have a business and a fan page. I will then jump onto YouTube to see if there is anything worthwhile from the channels I follow. However, I have to limit my time there to thirty minutes max. If you have ever been caught in the YouTube spiral, you know what I'm talking about. I can start watching a self-help video, and two hours later, I find myself watching videos about flat earthers or skinwalkers. It's crazy. Be sure to set a timer whenever you jump onto social media.

Always talk about what you are going to do . . . it's easier than actually doing it!

You likely know someone who is a big talker. They constantly talk about their big plans and projects and how successful they are going to be. They speak up and monopolize meetings and make sure that everyone knows their opinions and grandiose ideas. Yet, very few of these big talkers ever achieve anything significant in their lives. It's easy to talk about something. It is much more challenging to make that talk a reality.

A former client (we will call him Bob) came in to see me as he struggled with conflict in his relationships, specifically with his wife. During our very first session, Bob stated other people had told him that he is rude and opinionated. When I asked him if he agreed with the feedback, he said, "Not really. I'm always right." Bob spent most of our first session talking about how successful he was in his business, how he is looked up to as a leader, and his plan to be a millionaire by the time he was fifty years old. After many sessions with Bob and some forced introspection, Bob acknowledged that he really felt like a failure. His business was not nearly as successful as he had first stated. He realized that he was putting on a façade so that he wouldn't be judged or looked down upon. He was able to take a more objective view of his life and business, and Bob committed to making changes, the first being honest with himself.

Spend all of your time with negative and toxic people.

If you really want to guarantee failure, spend all your time with negative, toxic, and hateful people. They are easy to find. Just jump onto social media, and you are sure to find one in a matter of seconds. These individuals are very brave behind a keyboard and are leaders in criticizing and putting other people down.

These people could be friends or family. If they are friends, you need to take an honest look at why they are your friend. Maybe it is a friend you have had since high school, and you have taken different paths and no longer have things in common as you may have had when you were seventeen years old.

I had a best friend from elementary school through high school. We would hang out, talk about sports, played baseball together. I went on to college, and he served in the military, which is by no means a bad thing. The point is the trajectory of our lives went in different directions. We had less in common as we grew into adulthood. The length of time you have been friends with someone does not necessarily affect the strength of that relationship as you move forward in your life.

Here is a shocking truth for you. If you become successful, you will lose friends. Not everyone is going to support you or be happy for you. Many people will feel threatened by your success. Why, you ask? Because people are creatures of habit. They like routine and are uncomfortable with change. If you become successful, many of your friends will feel pressure to make positive changes in their own lives, which is challenging.

Over my years practicing therapy, I have worked with many people recovering from alcohol and drugs. You would think that friends of someone in recovery would be supportive, loving, and helpful. And many of those friends are. Some are not. Some friends will not like the change. They miss the "party" person that a person used to be. They may feel that they need to stop using, and this makes them uncomfortable. These people sometimes even try to sabotage recovery because they want things to stay the way they were.

What about family? Over the years, I have made this statement thousands of times to my clients. Just because it is family, it does not mean you HAVE to have a relationship with them. You don't get to choose your family. You are born into it. It is entirely possible that your family may not be good people. It is not okay if your parents, siblings, or other family members are negative and toxic. You can make a choice to disconnect and focus on your growth and success.

Toxic people come in many forms. You should avoid these people at all costs. This may involve removing yourself from long-standing relationships and even family members. Trust me when I say you will be better off without them.

- **The Gossiper** – A person who gossips derives pleasure from other people's misfortunes. This is not the type of person who will be supportive or happy for your success. A Spanish proverb states, "He who gossips to you will gossip about you."

- **The Victim** – The victim is constantly complaining about their own life and circumstances and blames everyone and everything except themselves for their position in life. They fail to take any responsibility for anything and choose to suffer to garner attention and sympathy from others.

- **The One Upper** – This individual constantly puts the focus on themselves instead of taking an interest in you and your achievements. The one-upper always has a story or an experience that will top yours, and they see everything as a competition. They will never be supportive because they are too busy talking about themselves. Constant interruptions and stories about themselves are what the One Upper thrives on.

- **The Liar** – This person is rarely, if ever, honest. They will make up stories and experiences and will never be truthful with you. They will tell you what you want to hear and have no interest in open, honest relationships.

Over promise and under deliver.

A sure-fire way to ensure your failure is to overpromise and underdeliver. When you fail to follow through on commitments, it depletes your credibility. People will not trust you, and your business and/or career will be doomed for failure.

I had a pool installed at my home last summer and was referred to a pool installer by the store where I purchased the pool. The installer inspected the area and promised that the pool would be installed quickly and efficiently. This did not happen. One panel on the backside of the pool was out of the track and bowed inward. The support posts were not properly attached. The installer blamed the shoddy work on a storm that came through while they were working. After dismantling and reinstalling the pool to my satisfaction, the installer mentioned a retaining wall.

Our yard slopes drastically toward the back fence to allow rain drainage away from the home. The installer never mentioned this when he originally quoted the job. The retaining wall installation was going to be $500 additional cost to what we already paid. Needless to say, I told him that his work was done and that I was going to hire someone else for the retaining wall project.

This guy overpromised and underdelivered. This is one of the worst mistakes a business can make. It leads to poor reviews, a bad reputation, and a lack of work going forward.

Procrastinate . . . always put yourself against the wall.

Let's talk about procrastination. Wait. Let's do that later. No, I'm joking. Procrastination is the single most powerful obstacle to your success. The word procrastination is derived from the Latin verb procrastinare, which means "to put off until tomorrow." Dr. Piers Steel, professor of motivational psychology at the University of Calgary, goes so far as to state procrastination is "self-harm." I am going to address procrastination in much greater detail in an upcoming chapter.

Absolutely refuse to ask for help when you need it.

Humans are hardwired to want to do things on their own. We like to take on tasks and accomplish them independently. When you ask for help from someone, it stirs up emotions like lack of confidence, low self-esteem, and acknowledging that you cannot do certain things independently.

The first home that my wife and I purchased after we were married was built in 1948. It had character. It also had many issues that needed fixing. Let me share first that I'm not a handyman. I had the grand idea to install a ceiling fan in our bedroom, which seemed simple enough. Take out the light fixture and install the ceiling fan. Sounds easy, right? Wrong. After removing the light fixture, I realized the electrical box in the ceiling was not the standard boxes used in modern construction. I thought to myself that I would simply remove that box and install a new one. It wasn't that easy. Long story short, I had to hire someone. I had to ask for help.

Not asking for help when you need it can have devastating repercussions. Yes, it may be a blow to your ego, but taking on something you are not qualified or have the ability to do can damage your professional reputation.

Another reason people do not ask for help is they believe they are imposing on others or that the person you are asking will say no. We don't like to impose on friends for family. We think it will just be easier to do it ourselves. Analyze the project and honestly evaluate if you have the knowledge and skill to accomplish the task.

Quit immediately if something doesn't work.

It might take one try to be successful. Most likely, it will take many tries. Failing at something can have devastating effects on your life and self-esteem, especially if you have a significant financial investment. You must learn from mistakes and failures. This will enable you to move forward with more knowledge and experience.

Sylvester Stallone is an excellent example of someone who did not give up. He was homeless as a young adult, living in a bus station. Later as an adult and while writing his script for *Rocky*, he was so broke his utilities were turned off, and he had to sell his dog just to get the power back on. Talent scouts rejected him over 1,500 times. Imagine if he had quit the first time he met a challenge or difficulty.

The journey to success is never a straight line. There are curves, setbacks, and alterations of trajectory. You must push through these detours to get back on track and keep moving closer to your end goal.

Here are some ways to keep yourself from quitting.

- **Remind yourself of your why.**

  We covered your why in the second chapter. This is the driving force for everything that you do. Print out your why and put it somewhere you will see it often (maybe on your desk at work or your office at home). This will remind you numerous times daily of what your why is.

- **Think about the progress you have already made.**

  If you quit, all the progress and lessons learned go to waste. You have spent time and effort to get where you are. Don't throw that away because of a challenge or difficulty.

- **Remind yourself that nothing worth doing comes easy.**

  Look at any successful person, and they will tell you story after story of their struggles getting to where they are now.

- **Get inspired by other successful people.**

  Every life lesson has been learned by someone. Use the experiences of other successful people to help you. Read their books and learn from those who have trudged through the same challenges and struggles you are experiencing. Let them inspire you to keep moving forward.

Don't read books.

If you want to fail, don't read—ever! Reading is the quickest way to gain free information and knowledge of the world and how things work. Most successful people have diligent reading habits.

- Warren Buffet, one of the richest men in the world, spends five to six hours a day reading different news sources. He states, "That's how knowledge works. It builds up like compound interest. All of you can do it, but I guarantee not many of you will do it."

- Bill Gates reads fifty books a year.

- Oprah Winfrey, whose book club has catapulted numerous authors to the *New York Times* bestseller list, called reading her "personal path to freedom."

- Mark Cuban, the owner of the Dallas Mavericks and entrepreneur, reads for three hours each and every day.

Reading does not always have to be business-related or self-help. A good novel will expand your vocabulary and imagination. Numerous studies have shown the benefits of reading, including reducing stress, improving language skills, increasing creativity, and living longer. A Yale study completed in 2016 followed 3,600 adults over the age of fifty. The study showed that people who reported reading books for at least thirty minutes per day lived nearly two years longer than those who didn't.

Chapter 4
Beliefs

Y ou may be feeling unsatisfied with your current place in life, which is why I am assuming you have probably picked up this book. It is okay to admit it, and there is no shame in trying to solve the problem. The shameful part is if you are hiding the pain and pretending that everything is okay.

What if I told you that change is just as simple as changing your beliefs? Would it bring you some satisfaction? Would it bring you peace or cause you even more worry?

There is no doubt that our beliefs are what impact our successes and failure in life. However, it may be difficult to accept this fact. This is precisely where the problem lies. If you don't believe it, you cannot change it.

Derren Brown is one of my favorite performers. He is known as a hypnotist, mentalist, magician, and motivational speaker. Derren Brown has a special on Netflix called *Miracle*. In it, he expresses one of the most influential theories on our belief system that I have ever heard. In this show, he states, "Don't tell yourself you are going to fail. That's just a story we tell ourselves. And this idea that our stories define us, in other words, it's really not events that affect us but more our reactions to them." This theory goes way back to the Roman philosopher Epictetus. Epictetus espoused a philosophy called Stoicism. Stoicism is a philosophy that focuses on positive emotions, reducing negative emotions, and emphasizing virtues of character.

I often emphasize to clients that you are only in control of two things in life: Your own thoughts and your own actions. That's it. Everything else that happens in the world is beyond your control. If you just let everything else go, you automatically become happier.

If you have never heard or watched any of Derren Brown's shows, I highly recommend viewing this one. It really will change the way you view yourself and your belief system.

I want to build on Derren's words and emphasize that we all tell ourselves stories. It has happened since we were self-aware at a very young age. We make up these stories based on events and experiences in our lives. When we were young children, we believed in Santa Claus.

We told ourselves that a man in a red suit would visit our homes and leave us presents under the tree on Christmas morning. We continued telling ourselves the same story every year until one day, the story changed.

At some point, that story no longer continued to be true. Had we continued to tell ourselves that same story into adulthood, you can imagine the issues that would cause. Imagine going to work on December 20th and talking with co-workers, "I can't wait for Santa to come in five days." The reactions would be entertaining. The point I want to emphasize is that this story changes for children based on new information. That additional information is that Santa Clause does not exist. It was a lie. And, had you continued to believe that lie, it would adversely affect your life as an adult.

We do the same things with many other lies that we tell ourselves, such as, "I'm not good enough"; "I'm not smart enough"; "I cannot do what other people can do"; "I don't have the ability to be successful." All these lies are based on what other people have told you. It could also be based on experiences of failure, feelings of low self-esteem, and other negative experiences in your life.

And these destructive thoughts, the stories we tell ourselves, often last into adulthood, affecting work, relationships and preventing you from achieving the success you are looking for.

Now that we are addressing beliefs, the stories we tell ourselves, I need you to pay attention to the piece of furniture you are sitting on as you read this book. It appears to be sturdy. It can hold your weight. It is performing just as it should be.

Are you aware right before you sat down to read this book, you had to make a snap decision? It was so fast that you probably were not even aware of it. Still, you made a decision. What was the decision? It was your assessment of the condition of that piece of furniture. This is a massive decision because if you had sat on a chair without thinking or considering whether it is sturdy enough to hold your weight or whether it is in the proper position, you could have fallen flat on the floor. You may have even hurt yourself.

Belief is the reason you sat down without even thinking about it. You believed that the chair would hold your weight. You believed that the chair is in good enough shape to take care of you and save you from any harm. But here is the crazy part. You never made the decision consciously. You don't stand around a chair asking yourself whether the chair will hold you or not (unless you are trying to sit in a plastic kids' chair). This process is done within a split second in the back of your mind.

This *back of your mind* I'm referring to is the subconscious mind where all your beliefs are stored. I realize that this is not physiologically accurate but imagine your mind had two compartments. The front part is your conscious mind. It's the part of your mind you are using right now to read this book. The *back* part is the subconscious mind. The subconscious mind is where all of your habits are stored, good or bad. The stories you tell yourselves are on a constant loop, and you are not even aware of the messages being reinforced in the subconscious mind.

I want to emphasize the point that belief is vital for your daily existence. You do it all the time. Your beliefs are what motivate you to operate. You live in belief. Belief is what ties your life together. It informs your decisions and makes your life possible.

If you believe that a particular chair can hold you up, then why do you believe in things that hold you down? If you are struggling in life, it is because you continue to believe in the things that prevent you from moving forward. You continuously tell yourself the same stories. These stories are based on the experiences of your past. They continue to strengthen the negative thought patterns and feelings of low-esteem and failure. .

Nobody wants to hear this because it leads to the ultimate conclusion that we all need to change. Change can be scary. Change is uncomfortable. Change is challenging. Without change, we are doomed to continue the same behaviors, thoughts, beliefs, and stories that we have always adhered to.

We are the authors of our own lives. We make that call. We make that decision, and nothing hurts more than coming face to face with the reality that we sometimes make bad choices. We make mistakes. We do things wrong. But if we continue to tell ourselves that same story over and over again, we continue to do the same thing over and over again.

If you are facing troubles in your relationships, your job, your health, your weight, and your appearance, it is all because you are living out of the stories that you tell yourself. No one likes being wrong. No one enjoys making mistakes. But the good news is that you can change!

You do not have to be trapped. Instead, you can tap into the power of belief so that you can make better decisions. You need to understand that the world does not care about your feelings. The world does not give a damn about your emotional state. What it pays attention to are your actions. You need to change your beliefs to make better decisions. You change your beliefs, and your actions follow.

The theme of my podcast—*The Motor City Hypnotist Podcast*—is "Change Your Thinking, Change Your Life." You choose your beliefs, and these are the foundation of your reality. They are the lenses that you use to filter reality. They are not forced on you. You have voluntarily assumed them. You always have a say.

I am not going to go on and bash media as a whole. However, there are some disturbing trends, and this influences adolescents and their belief systems. Much of the following information is taken from the website verywellfamily.com.

According to a report by Common Sense Media, the average teen spends about nine hours per day using media for their enjoyment. Frighteningly, it is likely same teens spend much less time a day talking to their parents. During hours of media consumption, teenagers are flooded with innumerable messages about the "ideal" body. These unrealistic and unattainable portrayals of beauty can wreak havoc on adolescent's body image (verywellfamily.com).

Movies, commercials, magazines, and websites portray beautiful people as ideal. Underweight models and photoshopped images of perfection are everywhere. Diet products and beauty items send the message that being thinner and more attractive is the key to happiness and success.

The effect can be seen in children at a young age. Research shows children as young as age three prefer game pieces that depict thin people over those representing heavier ones. And by age ten, 80% of American girls have been on a diet.

It is not just traditional media that places teens under pressure to be thin and beautiful. Social media may have an even more powerful effect on adolescents' body image. Many teens seek validation from their peers, and social media is the quickest and easiest way to gain feedback. Whether a teen posts a selfie on Instagram, or he/she views pictures of others boasting about their "summer body" on Snapchat, social influences can be compelling.

Some teens spend hours trying to capture a selfie at just the right angle. Others gauge their appearance based on how many likes their latest Facebook photo receives. The immediate, peer-to-peer feedback can be addictive for those whose self-esteem depends on social media affirmations. Unfortunately, many teens receive harsh criticism and rude comments on social media. I see many adolescent clients in my practice. Cyberbullying is a significant challenge for teenagers and can substantially negatively affect a teen's body image.

This pressure to be "ideal" can have serious repercussions. Research has linked images of underweight air-brushed female bodies to unhealthy eating habits and decreased self-esteem. In a survey conducted by Girlguiding, half of girls ages sixteen to twenty-one said they would undergo surgery to improve their bodies.

Poor body image can lead to even more severe consequences. While some teens develop eating disorders, others experience depression. A 2009 study by verywellfamily.com, found that girls who were unhappy with their appearance were at a significantly higher risk for suicide.

It is not just females who are subjected to unrealistic media portrayals of beauty. Boys are bombarded with images of six-pack abs and big muscles. Superheroes and action figures depict these unrealistic body types and start sending boys the wrong messages at a young age. The pursuit of the perfect body takes a toll on boys. Teen boys may strive for the ideal body by dieting or through compulsive exercise. They may also develop eating disorders or mental health problems stemming from poor body image, as reported on icyf.org.

These beliefs or "stories" that teens tell themselves often continue into adulthood and can cause self-esteem and confidence issues. It is challenging to change these stories when they have been embedded repeatedly during adolescence. The great news is that by changing your beliefs, changing the stories you tell yourself, you can achieve a new self-confidence and success level.

Psychology Today has some great insight into your belief systems and how the stories you tell yourself can affect you. Your emotional memory has accumulated an incredible amount of data to inform and protect you if you encounter a similar situation in the future. How fortunate it is that the next time you encounter a problem—one that is similar to a previous event where emotion was activated—your emotional memory will be able to recall what you experienced and respond accordingly.

The ability of the human brain to compare current experiences to the stored representations of previous experiences is referred to as "pattern matching" (Nathanson, 1992). Psychology Today offers that, at times, emotional memories that are based on your previous experiences may lead you to develop cognitive beliefs that may be contrary to your goals or interfere with them.

For example, you are in search of an intimate and loving relationship. However, you have a belief that you are unlovable and flawed. Therefore, you avoid any close contact with others.

Experiencing yourself as being unlovable or flawed does not translate directly to emotional memories where one made you feel unloved or flawed. Instead, the foundation of such emotions is related to shame. Emotional memories and their impact on our beliefs can be complex.

The most effective way to change emotional beliefs is to change how you think about these emotions. Emotions are a vital component of being human. Without them, we are unable to love, to feel close to someone, to enjoy happiness. However, when emotions are left to control without a healthy established belief system, it can affect us negatively, making it difficult to experience success and happiness.

I am not saying that you need to eradicate emotions. For any of my fellow Star Trek fans, Mr. Spock would purport that logic should supersede emotion. Fortunately, or sometimes, unfortunately, we cannot dismiss emotion. There has to be a balance. Because you may have been hurt emotionally in the past does not mean that the same story exists for you in the present.

When you limit your beliefs, you limit your possibilities for success. Some examples of limiting one's beliefs include:

- **"It's hard to make money these days."**

   You will not push yourself to the limit to make money because you believe that hard work is not worth it because it is not easy to make money.

- **"Relationships are too complicated."**

This belief will limit your relationships. If you believe that relationships are complicated, you will not seek a relationship. You will prepare yourself to feel lonely, even though deep down, you are searching for someone with whom to share your life.

- **"Risk is dangerous."**

If you believe this, you will never attempt to start anything new because you fear that you will fail. And if you do not try anything, there is no chance for you to be successful.

- **"I'm not like successful people. I don't have the personality."**

You may not be comfortable in conducting sales, so you may not be the top salesperson. However, there are many other ways to be successful. You need to base your goals and your aspirations on your strengths and your abilities.

Your belief has an impact on your expectations and assumptions. Start from there. What is that you assume about yourself that is correct? Is it your life, your place in the world, or your capabilities? What is it that you expect out of your life?

In the same way you adopt certain beliefs, you can drop them. Belief affects your way of handling situations. It affects how you cope with problems. Know that belief does work and that belief is a choice. Choose better beliefs, and you will get better results. It is that simple. The most effective way to change those subconscious beliefs is through hypnosis. I cannot wait to share that with you in a later chapter.

Chapter 5
Remove Limiting Beliefs

There are many moments in life when something unexpected occurs. These unexpected events may be unremarkable, tragic, or optimistic. When you experience something sudden and different, it leaves an imprint on your memory. The Collins Dictionary definition states, "If something leaves an imprint on a place or your mind, it has a strong and lasting effect on it." The additional definition (used as a transitive verb) states, "When something is imprinted on your memory, it is firmly fixed in your memory so that you will not forget it."

You can imagine that tragic events are often imprinted in memories, especially if an individual is a victim or eyewitness of a tragic event. These imprints can also occur from a distance, for example, watching a sad event on television. For those of you who are old enough to remember the 9/11 tragedy, I am sure we can all agree that it left an indelible imprint on our minds. The scenes and sounds of that day have been permanently imprinted in our minds, and we can willingly or unwillingly play those scenes out repeatedly.

One of the most severe results of imprinted memories takes the form of Post-Traumatic Stress Disorder. The Mayo Clinic states, "post-traumatic stress disorder (PTSD) is a mental health condition that's triggered by a terrifying event—either experiencing it or witnessing it. Symptoms may include flashbacks, nightmares, and severe anxiety, as well as uncontrollable thoughts about the event."

I have treated many clients over the years that suffer from symptoms of PTSD. Those symptoms include:

- Unwanted, recurring distressing memories of the traumatic event

- Flashbacks causing the victim to relive the traumatic event as if it were happening again

- Nightmares and upsetting dreams about the traumatic event

- Severe emotional and physical reactions to events or things that remind you of the traumatic event

- Avoidance of thinking or discussing the event

- Avoiding people, places, or activities that remind you of the traumatic event

- Negative thoughts about yourself, other people, or the world

- Feelings of hopelessness about the future

- Memory and recall issues, especially about details surrounding the traumatic event

- Inability to maintain relationships and feeling detached and distant from family and friends

- Lack of interest in hobbies or activities you once enjoyed

- Feeling emotionally numb

- Difficulty experiencing positive emotions

- Being easily startled by sounds or other people

- Difficulty sleeping or concentrating

- Feeling irritable

- Experiencing angry outbursts

- Deep feelings of guilt or shame

While this is not an exhaustive list, it does represent many difficulties people with PTSD struggle with.

In November of 2013, I was driving to my office to see clients. I had some evening appointments, so I left my home at around 5:00 pm to see clients starting at 6:00 pm. It was already dark. I was driving on a four-lane road separated by a double yellow line. There was no turn lane on this street, and I was in the left lane, just adjacent to the double yellow. I was traveling about forty-five miles an hour which was the speed limit. I approached a vehicle traveling in the opposite direction, just on the other side of the separator. I came upon it quickly as I realized the vehicle was not moving. It was stopped in the opposite lane. Just as I was passing, the vehicle door opened, and a man stepped in front of my car. It was so fast yet almost felt like slow motion at the same time. I remember thinking, "Oh my God! I'm going to hit this guy!" just as all hell broke loose inside my vehicle and my mind. The front left of my car hit him, propelling him into my windshield and then down the side of my car. A cloud of breaking glass swirled around me as my heart felt like it was jumping out of my throat, and there was a moment of disconnect in my brain. It was as if I just disappeared from reality for that split second of time and was blank. I immediately pulled over, and a rush of adrenaline took over. I could not think, move or act. My mind had a hundred thoughts at once. I was shaking so badly; I could barely open my door.

This was a traumatic event. This event shocked my system and left an indelible imprint on my mind that still exists today.

The gentleman lived, thank goodness. Long story short, he had been rear-ended by another vehicle and exited his vehicle to assess the damage, unaware of his surroundings or proximity to traffic coming in the opposite direction (namely me).

Our history and experiences are recorded in our minds. The experiences that are the most shocking, traumatic, or even joyful or inspirational are in our permanent record. They do not drop off after seven years like a bad debt on your credit report. These recordings are always accessible and, sometimes, play automatically.

Now you do not have to experience trauma like the one I described above to have recurring unwanted memories. Something as simple as being criticized as a child can have long-lasting effects that can last into adulthood. Maybe a bad relationship you had when you were twenty-two years old still affects how you interact with possible partners in your forties. These experiences and memories have become your life movie. And just like any other movie, you most likely watch it passively, seemingly without the ability to change it.

If you recall back to your childhood, your

curiosity may have allowed you to do things that you would not think of doing today. As kids, there are fewer self-imposed limits. Luckily, we had parents and caretakers that set the boundaries to keep us safe. A child might not think twice about touching a hot stove because he/she has no imprinted memories about hot stoves and what that would feel like. We are much braver as children than we are as adults.

There was a large hill for sledding in the city I grew up in. It was right behind the civic center and adjacent to the little league baseball fields I played on. It was a good-sized hill and had a six-foot fence separating the sledding part of the hill from the other side, a sharp decline that leveled off far below for about ten feet or so, then a drop into a deep ravine (which was probably ten feet deep). Being the sometimes-dumb kid I was, I accepted a challenge from my friends to climb the fence and sled down the other side. I was scared, but I also did not want to shy away from a challenge. I climbed over, laid face forward on my sled, and took off! I was instantly traveling at the speed of light (or so it felt), the freezing wind blowing my red cheeks. As the bottom of the decline approached very quickly, I suddenly realized that the ten feet of level ground at the bottom was nowhere near enough space to stop my speeding, out-of-control sled. I hit the edge going full speed and found myself weightless . . . and then in free fall. BAM. I hit the bottom of the ravine and saw stars.

The wind was knocked out of me, and I lay there struggling to breathe, my body feeling like it had been pummeled. After a few moments of agony, my breathing came back to normal, and I re-evaluated my ten-year-old life.

That experience, while painful, was valuable. It taught me not to be stupid. Unfortunately, it also imprinted on my mind that I should be scared and not take risks. This is a double-sided coin. Our childhood often teaches us that risk is wrong and that you will get hurt. As we move into adulthood, this could prevent us from taking risks or doing something that we perceive as dangerous (such as starting a business, taking a new position, investing money, buying a house).

Let me share one quick story. My grandparents used to often take my brother and me camping during the summers. They belonged to a camping club, and most summers, we would spend many weekends with them at different campgrounds. We were always so excited for these trips as we would get to sleep in a tent, eat outside at a picnic table, sit around a vast, roaring campfire every night making smores and playing with the other kids. On one of these weekend excursions, my brother and I were walking through the campground. We noticed a dog at one of the campsites. He was attached to a chain that was tied to a tree.

At home, we had a dog that was with us since I was five years old. Inky was her name. My dad brought her home as a birthday gift for my older sister, but Inky was our family pet. We played with her, wrestled with her, snuggled with her. We had imprinted memories about our dog and her behavior. My brother approached the dog at this campsite, and as he would often do with Inky. He went to kiss this dog on the head when the dog suddenly snapped and bit my brother in the face. Luckily, it was a superficial wound, and simple first aid addressed it. My brother learned something that day. He had new information imprinted in his mind that would shape his behaviors in the future. Well, at least I hoped so (sorry, brother).

The movie of our life influences every decision we make, and our experiences make our movies. Unfortunately, that movie is sometimes inaccurate. The movie replays all of our disappointments, failures, and hurt. This prevents us from "letting go" and challenging our status quo as adults. Your movie will often reinforce your limiting beliefs.

Lifehack.com states, "A limiting belief is a state of mind, a conviction or a belief that you think is true, and it limits you in some way. This belief could be about you, your interactions with others, or with the world as you know it. Limiting beliefs can keep you from making the right choices, taking on new opportunities, and ultimately reaching your potential." A great example of this comes from a client I was working with, whom we will call Jill. She had a string of unhealthy relationships. She had bounced from one guy to another over the course of a few years, and all of these relationships ended badly. There was a commonality to all of the guys she dated. They all treated her poorly. The guys all spoke poorly of her, dismissed her thoughts and feelings, and overall treated her like crap. Why would she continue to find guy after guy who treated her poorly? Because she had a faulty belief that she was not worth being treated well. Her limiting belief was, "I'm not good enough to be treated well."

Your beliefs have negative as well as positive consequences in your life. Beliefs affect your moods, relationships, self-esteem, job performance, physical health, and even your religion. Beliefs can be conscious, as well as subconscious. Like a hard drive in the computer, this is where your belief system is stored. And like computer memory, the data is stored in the energy field surrounding the central processing chip.

What happens if the beliefs stored in that computer memory or movie that you replay over and over again are false? False beliefs are beliefs that we have about others and things that are untrue. They reside in our subconscious mind as a result of our experiences. Because 90% of our actions come from our subconscious, our false beliefs play a huge role in almost everything we do. And because these beliefs reside in our subconscious, we are not aware of them and how they affect us.

For example, if you believe that you are unlovable, you may tend to sabotage relationships. If you feel incapable of specific skills and abilities, you may turn down a job promotion or a different position. Medium.com states, "Our behavior comes from our beliefs. And our life is shaped by our responses. Therefore, if we change our beliefs, especially false ones, we can change our behavior and life."

So how do you identify those limiting beliefs? If they reside in your subconscious, how do you root them out and determine if they are holding you back? I am going to share some strategies to identify your own limiting beliefs.

1. The *Third Person* Method

Sometimes it is much easier to see faults in others. Hop on Facebook for just ten minutes, and you will know what I am talking about. In this method, examine someone you know who may have limiting beliefs. It could be a friend who hates their job and continuously makes excuses about why they cannot change careers or look for another job. Examine them from the outside and observe how limiting beliefs affect their happiness and self-worth. Try looking from the outside and applying those thoughts and evaluations to your situation.

2. The *Fill-in-the-Blank* Method

List or say a situation out loud that you are struggling with and then say the word "because." For example, "I am miserable in my relationship *because* . . ." Then write down all of the reasons you are unhappy. For example, "I am miserable in my relationship *because* . . . I don't feel appreciated."

3. The *I Can't* Method

Think of all of the things in your life when you said, "I can't." List down all of the things that you think you cannot do or achieve. Once you have that list ready, add the reasons why you cannot do those things. For example, "I can't speak in front of people." The reasons might be fear, lack of confidence, poor voice, and your belief that you will fail if you tried. Then write down what you would do to correct each reason. If your reason is a lack of confidence, you can address it with practice and experience. Just as Henry Ford stated long ago, "Whether you think you can, or you think you cannot, you're right."

4. The *I Don't Have* Method

People use this rationalization why they are not

able to achieve a goal or complete a task. You will have heard these or maybe even said them yourself. "I don't have the talent"; "I don't have the money"; "I don't have the time"; "I don't have the confidence"; "I don't have the knowledge"; "I don't have the motivation." We use built-in excuses to justify why we are not successful and why others experience more success than we do. List each of your "don't haves" and then write a possible solution for each one. If you "don't have the time," then write down a set schedule or ways to free up fifteen minutes in your day.

Take a few minutes and write down any and all of your limiting beliefs. Some may exist from childhood. Some may have developed in adulthood. Use the techniques listed above to reframe those limiting beliefs. Once the limitations are removed, your potential becomes unlimited.

Chapter 6
The Problem of Procrastination

Like many, I was an expert procrastinator. My procrastination issues go way back to my college days. I was the student who was up all night studying for a final exam or plunking the keys of my typewriter at 6:00 am to finish a paper due for my 8:00 am class. And yes, I did say typewriter!

What is procrastination? The word comes from the Latin term *pro-crastinus* which means "belonging to tomorrow." Merriam-Webster has two definitions for procrastination.

Transitive Verb: to put off intentionally and habitually.

Intransitive Verb: to put off intentionally the doing of something that should be done.

You will notice that both definitions use the word intentionally. You may feel like delaying or putting something off is beyond your control. But, by definition, your actions are intentional. Thinking back to those all-nighters in college, it sure did not feel like it was intended. And there lies the problem. Just like any other bad habit, procrastination becomes a way of life. It may not be something you consciously choose to do, but you are choosing to do it.

If you have ever been pushed to a deadline or have something that needed to be completed, only to be scrambling at the last minute to finish the task, you know it just does not feel good. It brings on feelings of anxiety, pressure, and often depression. So that brings up the million-dollar question. Why?

Why Do People Procrastinate?

People will often assume that procrastinators are lazy, unmotivated individuals. They may be looked upon with disdain by the "go-getter" and those that get things done. This is an unfair evaluation because there is a scientific and psychological cause for procrastination. As any procrastinator will tell you, they will complete the task or assignment when it needs to be done. When you are faced with a task to complete, you are now obligated to do something. It could be at home or work, but we humans have a difficult time with obligations. Doing something that you want to do is much more fun than doing something you *have* to do. Therein lies the psychological disconnect. We would much rather be doing something fun than completing an obligation.

There are also times when we become demotivated. Anxiety, fear, and many other negative emotions cause us to lack the motivation to take action. I was working with a client who I will call Bob. Bob worked at a corporate job and was always expressing how overwhelmed he felt. He acknowledged that his work was never recognized and that he thought he was being taken for granted. Bob's interest in completing tasks and work assignments were low. He was dealing with feelings of frustration and anger because he felt his work was not being recognized. After more than a few sessions with Bob, our discussion eventually revealed that Bob had been written up due to his poor performance in the past; written up numerous times over his years with the company. Bob finally acknowledged that he felt inadequate and lacked the confidence to do his job at a high level. You can imagine that it would be hard for Bob to be motivated, which led to chronic procrastination. Bob eventually agreed to discuss with his manager, express his feelings to her, and acknowledge his shortcomings. After that discussion, Bob gradually became more confident, responsible and, believe it or not, started enjoying his job.

Procrastination is also a habit. We have talked about habits a lot in this book, which is another example of subconscious thinking patterns influencing behaviors. If someone has procrastinated since they were a child, why should we expect that person to be any different as an adult? People procrastinate because it is something they have most likely always done.

Another reason people may procrastinate is that they do not see value in the task at hand. If you must do something and do not believe it is necessary, chances are you will put that thing off as long as possible.

Causes of Procrastination

Assuming procrastination is a habit developed from early childhood, how is it reinforced into adulthood? Some of these factors contribute significantly to the issue.

- **Delayed rewards.**

  People will often put off tasks that do not provide an immediate reward or satisfaction. As a homeowner, one of the tasks I dislike the most is mowing my lawn. I know that once the task is completed, my yard will look better, and my dog will not have to use the bathroom in grass that is up to his stomach. Even having that information, I find it challenging to get motivated to do it. If someone were standing in my backyard holding a hundred-dollar bill and said, "as soon as you cut the grass, this is yours," I would be much more motivated to throw on my yard clothes and mow the grass.

- **Unable to see our future.**

Many of us procrastinate because we are unable to see our future selves after the task has been completed. There is a phenomenon called *temporal self-discontinuity.* Many clients come into my office for hypnotherapy to stop smoking. I am sure if you are or were a smoker, your doctor has undoubtedly told you that you need to stop as the habit will cause a myriad of health issues in your future. Yet, most people continue to smoke because their future self is disconnected from their present reality. In a sense, they view their future selves as different people. This thinking leads people to continue their current bad habits and assume their "future self" will deal with it when the time comes.

- **Indecisiveness.**

People will often put things off because they cannot decide which course of action to take. You may delay changing your eating habits because you cannot determine the best approach to bring you the most effective changes. If you have a large project for school, you may put off starting it as you cannot decide what topic you want to cover.

Numerous factors lead to indecisiveness. The more options that are available, the more difficult it will be to choose. Imagine walking into your nearest Baskin Robbins and having only chocolate or vanilla to choose from as opposed to twenty different flavors. The more choices you have, the more complex the choice becomes, resulting in procrastination.

If you have similar choices, it also becomes more difficult to choose. If you are looking at two dresses which are both shades of blue, the decision is much more difficult than if the colors were opposite.

If you are making an important choice, it will be more challenging to choose. The greater the possible consequences, the more your mind struggles to make the "right" decision.

- **Being overwhelmed.**

When faced with several tasks to complete rather than just one item, we become overwhelmed and often don't know where to begin. I have clients who are constantly "behind" on duties and tasks at home as there are so many things to do, it is easier to do nothing at all.

- **Fear of failure.**

People will often put off tasks because they fear failure. I had a client that we will call Joe. Joe had been working at his job for over ten years but was miserable. He told me he would get up each day, dreading going to work. He would often experience stomach issues, headaches, and fatigue because he hated his job. We often talked about possibly changing jobs or even pursuing a career in a different field. Joe's typical response was "What if it doesn't work?" or "What if I fail at a new job?" Joe was resistant to making change because he was fearful of the unknown. He finally pursued a job change after many weeks of therapy and was much happier as a result.

The Effects of Procrastination

You may be thinking to yourself, "So what if I wait until the last minute as long as the thing gets completed." Fair enough. Most procrastinators do end up completing the project, task, or work. And any true procrastinator will rationalize and say, "That's how I work," or "I work better under pressure," or "I always meet my deadlines." While all of these statements may be true, what is the cost to an individual who is a habitual procrastinator?

A study was completed in 2015 by Dr. Fuschia M. Sirois from Bishops University in Canada. In his research, he found that chronic procrastination is associated with a myriad of adverse mental health and physical consequences, including depression, anxiety, illnesses such as colds and flu, and life-threatening issues including cardiovascular disease. The constant pressure of pushing deadlines to the last minute or waiting until your "back is against the wall" causes undue stress and can have a significant impact on your health.

The big question is, "What do I do if I'm a procrastinator?" While there are many answers to this question, the most basic and simple answer is to get started. We will discuss motivation in the next chapter.

Chapter 7
Motivation

Scientists describe motivation as the overall willingness to do something. It is the compilation of emotional and cognitive forces that compels someone to take some action.

So, what specifically is motivation? A quote by Steven Pressfield from his novel, *The War of Art*, sums up in a nutshell motivation and procrastination, "At some point, the pain of not doing it becomes greater than the pain of doing it."

This is the essence of motivation. Every choice has a cost, but it is easier to overcome the inconvenience of action when we are motivated than the distress of staying the same. We cross a mental threshold— typically after procrastination and in the face of an urgent deadline— and it becomes much more painful not to do the task than to do it. Now for the critical issue: what can we do to increase the likelihood that we will break this mental barrier and feel compelled regularly?

One of the most shocking things about motivation is that it often comes after a new behavior starts, not before. Author James Clear puts it this way: "I like to refer to this effect as the Physics of Productivity because this is Newton's First Law applied to habit formation: objects in motion tend to remain in motion. Once you begin a task, it is easier and faster to keep moving it forward."

Nearly all the resistance with a task will be at the start. Progress comes more naturally after you start. During a discussion about developing products, one of my colleagues said to me, "Most people never do anything because they're always pondering what to do and how they are going to do it." The same paralysis applies to working out, starting a project, creating content, and building a business.

- If you don't have a fixed time to work out every day, then you'll wake up thinking each day, hoping to feel motivated to work out.

- If your business doesn't have a marketing system, then you'll arrive at your job just hoping that you'll find a way to market (in addition to all your other responsibilities).

- If you don't schedule a specific day and time to do something, you will find yourself saying over and over again, "I need to get this project started," and nothing will happen.

- If you don't have a planned time to write each week, then you'll find yourself saying, "I just need to find the self-discipline to do it," and it doesn't happen.

Don't wait for motivation to strike you. Your habits must be scheduled.

- Maya Angelou would go to a rented hotel room to write. She arrived at 6:30 am, wrote until 2:00 pm, and then went home to do some editing. She never slept at the hotel.

- Pulitzer Prize-winner Michael Chabon writes five nights per week from 10:00 pm to 3:00 am.

- Stephen King stated, *"I have a glass of water or a cup of tea. There's a certain time I sit down, from 8:00 [am] to 8:30 [am], somewhere within that half-hour every morning. I have my vitamin pill and my music, sit in the same seat, and the papers are all arranged in the same place. The cumulative purpose of doing these things the same way every day seems to be a way of saying to the mind, you're going to be dreaming soon."*

- C.S. Lewis would wake up at 8:00 am every morning, have breakfast, and write from 9:00 am to 1:00 pm.

The strength of a ritual, or what could be called a pre-game routine, is that it makes it simpler to start your habits, and that makes it easier to follow through consistently.

What Can Destroy Motivation?

- **Believing that you have to be perfect.**

Perfectionism can be the single most potent quality that can derail your motivation. Perfectionism is defined as the need or desire to be perfect or to achieve perfection. Perfection does not exist. It is unrealistic and unattainable. Yet many of us choose to try to be perfect, and if we cannot be perfect, we give up. This will destroy any plans or achievements that you may be capable of reaching.

I had a roommate during my freshman year of college. I won't share his name here just in case he miraculously ends up with my book in his hands. He was a junior at the time. Up to that point, he had all As throughout his entire school career. From first grade to his junior year in college, all As. He would attend class during the day and return to our dorm room to study until dinner time. We would head over to the student center for dinner, and upon returning to our room, he again would study until 11:00 pm or so and go to bed. This was his routine *every day*.

We had a conversation during one of those late-night study sessions just before Christmas break, and he expressed that he felt like he was "missing out" on college. Academically, he was an absolute success. However, he did not have a social life and spent extraordinarily little time outside our dorm room.

Upon returning in January for our spring semester, he confided in me that he had decided to start enjoying himself. We began going out for meals and attending campus parties. He started socializing and having fun. He was a much happier person. He was also a brilliant dude. His grades didn't tank. He still ended up with a very high grade point average, but he received a couple of B grades for the first time in his life. Once this happened, he said he felt free from the pressure he had been experiencing most of his life to be perfect academically. The world didn't end, and he wasn't banned from school for getting a couple of Bs. He was able to let go of his perfectionism and still be proud of his accomplishments.

- **Not resting.**

Are you a Type-A personality? Are you a person constantly driven to succeed and never take breaks or time for yourself?

In her book, *The Sleep Revolution,* Arianna Huffington shared that she experienced a massive wake-up call when she woke up on the floor of her office in a pool of her blood. She had collapsed and hit her face, breaking her cheekbone. She was diagnosed with exhaustion. She acknowledges in her book that she was consistently working eighteen-hour days and trying to do it all. She is now committed to getting eight hours of sleep per night.

The Mayo Clinic recommends that adults get between seven and nine hours of sleep per night. The website Sciencedaily.com states, "In the United States, the average American sleeps less than the minimum seven hours of sleep per night recommended by the Center for Disease Control, and nearly half of Americans report negative consequences from insufficient sleep. This problem appears to be especially prevalent in men, who report getting significantly less sleep, on average, than women."

You must have an established sleep schedule that ensures you get seven to nine hours of sleep per night. Sleep deprivation will harm your motivation and your ability to accomplish goals.

- **A full plate.**

Being able to focus on one thing at a time helps you organize and prioritize your objectives. Having too much to do and multi-tasking will cause undue stress and anxiety and will likely be unfulfilling. It is essential to prioritize your tasks in order of importance and focus on one thing at a time. This will enable you to make progress, and as you see your progress, it enhances your motivation to do more.

Be sure to set limits and healthy boundaries with other people. You may have those people in your life that tend to take and never give. If you continually say yes to these people, you will most likely end up being resentful and unhappy.

Steps To Get Motivated

Step 1: Make the first steps easy. For example, your writing routine might begin with a few minutes of mindful meditation. Or your workout routine may start with some simple stretching exercises. The beginning is the most significant component of any task. In the beginning, if you cannot get motivated, you will discover that motivation often comes after you start. That is why you need to make your pre-game routine relatively easy.

Step 2: Your routine should move you toward your ultimate objective. There is often a lack of mental motivation associated with an absence of physical motion. Imagine your physical condition when you feel depressed, bored, or unmotivated. Your physiology dictates your mental state. Take a moment to stand, shout, do a little dance—anything to get your body moving. You will find your mental state improves when you change your physiology. As you start your routine with easy steps, begin moving into more complex or challenging steps gradually. Your mental state will match your physical state. If you sit down to write, maybe take ten seconds to stretch your arms, breathe deeply in and out and then begin.

Step 3: Do the exact same things every time! The primary purpose of your routine is to create a series of actions that you complete *every time* before starting your tasks. This routine eventually becomes so linked to your performance that you are drawn into a mental state that is prepared to perform by simply doing the routine. You do not have to try to be motivated. Just begin your routine, and the motivation will follow.

James Clear's Three Rs of Motivation

1) Reminder – The trigger that precedes the habit (example: traffic light turns green).

2) Routine – The action you take. The habit itself (example: you drive through the intersection).

3) Reward – The result from doing the task (example: you get closer to your destination).

The Goldilocks Principal

The Goldilocks principle is named for an analogy to the children's story, *The Three Bears*. A girl named Goldilocks tastes three different bowls of porridge and finds that she prefers porridge that is neither too hot nor too cold but has just the right temperature. Since the children's story is well known across cultures, the concept of "just the right amount" is easily understood and applies to motivation. Imagine you are participating in a one-on-one competition (such as table tennis). If your opponent is a young child who is unskilled at table tennis, you will quickly lose interest as there is no real competition. If you were playing the world champion of table tennis, you would also quickly lose interest as you have little to no chance of winning. Compare these experiences to playing against someone who has a skill set that is close to or equal to your own. The game is much more likely to be competitive, with each person winning and losing some points. You have a chance to win the game if you are giving your total effort. You face a "just manageable" challenge.

The task you face is manageable. You may win or lose, but the process itself keeps you engaged because you have an excellent chance to win. Activities like these are more likely to keep us motivated in the long run. People enjoy challenges, but only if they are within the ideal difficulty range. Activities that are well below your skill level will fail to keep your interest. Activities that are well beyond your skill level will cause discouragement. But activities right on the edge of success and failure motivate our minds. The Goldilocks Rule states that humans experience peak motivation when working on tasks that are right on the edge of their current abilities. Not too hard. Not too easy. Just right (jamesclear.com).

One of the keys to keeping long-term motivation is working on assignments that conform to the Goldilocks Rule. If you feel unmotivated to work on a job, it is often because it has faded into a boredom zone or has been driven into "a too difficult" area. You need to discover a way to engage in tasks where you feel challenged but competent.

We can conclude that measurement is the primary motivating force. To put it more clearly, two of the most critical parts of peak motivation are tackling an ideal challenge and getting instant feedback on the progress you are making on that challenge.

Associate with Successful People

Who do you associate with? Who are your closest relationships (both personally and professionally)? These relationships will tell you a lot about your level of motivation and your possible future success.

Tony Robbins has long emphasized the importance of surrounding yourself with the people who practice the qualities you are aiming for. He states, "If we surround ourselves with people who are successful, who are forward-moving, who are positive, who are focused on producing results, who will support us, it will challenge us to be more and do more and share more... If you surround yourself with successful, forward-thinking people, it is much more likely for you to take on those qualities and start thinking and behaving just like them. Imagine being surrounded by positive, supportive people and how that would change the way you think and feel about yourself.

Think about the people with who you have the closest relationships. Identify the people you associate with the most and ask yourself the following questions. Please write down your answers for each one.

Do they support you?

Do they have the same professional goals as you?

Do they subscribe to the same work ethic as you?

Do you feel challenged when you are with them?

Do they encourage you to achieve and succeed?

We constantly have inner dialogue in our minds. That dialogue may say, *This is too difficult,* or *My writing is just not that good.* When that happens, rewrite that inner dialogue. Even say it out loud if you have to. Correct these negative thought patterns to become positive affirmations. When you have made progress on a task, tell yourself that you have accomplished something great. With each step of the process, reward yourself mentally for the work you have completed. When you do this over and over, you build a successful identity which leads to more success.

Chapter 8
The Secrets of Scheduling

What do you want for dinner? I don't know, what do you want? How about Italian? No. I'm not in the mood for Italian. How about Mexican. No. I'm not feeling like Mexican tonight. So please tell me what you want. I'm not sure.

How often has your family had this conversation? The back and forth about what to eat for dinner and when you finally decide, it might be an hour later, and you end up just settling for fast food or whatever you can find in your refrigerator. I am reminded of school days. Remember the lunch menu that your mom posted on your refrigerator? You never had to guess or figure out what you were going to have for lunch. Friday was always pizza day at my high school. It was the most looked forward to lunch each week. They would also have a peanut butter bar coated with chocolate on the tray. This was valuable currency in high school. Maybe more than cigarettes in prison.

We learned a lot in high school, and even some things we were not aware of could be beneficial into adulthood. What would happen if you made a dinner menu each week and posted it on your refrigerator at home? Monday might be spaghetti. Tuesday would, of course, be tacos. Wednesday might be burgers. You get the idea. You could refer to this menu when you do your grocery shopping each week, ensuring you have all the items needed for your meals. There would be no back and forth about what you are having for dinner each day. There is a plan in place that would help you manage time and ensure a consistent routine. This demonstrates the power of scheduling.

Do you struggle with getting things accomplished? Do you feel like you are always running on a treadmill and getting nowhere? Are you constantly feeling overwhelmed with responsibilities and feel like you never have a break? What would help you feel like you can manage all the tasks you have to do without feeling overwhelmed and out of control?

Scheduling. It sounds trite and cliché, but we will discuss the power of scheduling and how it can drastically reduce your stress level and give you a sense of accomplishment and satisfaction.

The definition of scheduling from Oxford is "to arrange or plan (an event) to take place at a particular time." Think about this for a moment and imagine a day filled with no planning, arranging, or scheduling events. What would that day look and feel like? Most likely, you think it would be chaos, and you would be correct. Without structure, we are doomed to meander along with no real purpose or plan. This is not a great way to approach life, a job, a career, or a business.

Scheduling sounds simple. Assuming that is true, why do most of us not implement schedules to manage our daily routines? It would certainly keep us on track and help us accomplish all the tasks we need to complete.

It makes you feel busier.

The more items you have on your schedule or to-do list, the busier you will feel. That psychological resistance keeps you from managing the schedule and completing tasks. The truth is, you are not any more active than you would be without the schedule. You are just not accustomed to seeing all of your jobs in front of you in print (or on your cell phone). It is better to have all of your tasks organized and scheduled than to work through your days without a clear vision of what needs to be done.

When I was in high school and college, Franklin Planners were a big deal. For all you youngsters out there, this was well before computers and cell phones. People actually carried around a physical book with pages of paper in it. We would use this ancient relic to write down appointments, take notes, and organize our to-do lists. I know. It sounds barbaric, doesn't it? If you want to verify the existence of this long-lost artifact from the past, Franklin Planner still has an active website, and you can order planners and page refills.

The world has moved on. We are now almost exclusively attached to cell phones wherever we go. We have calendars and note-taking apps on our phones. We have sharable calendars to make meetings and appointments easier. Yet, there still exists a disconnect from the real world to the electronic world. I have a theory that may explain this.

Back in the olden days, referenced last chapter, we carried our planners with us. We could refer to it whenever we needed to, and this helped us stay organized. However, no one could contact you on your Franklin Planner. There was no screen, no sound, no connection to the outside world. You could not open up your planner and browse for information about the airspeed velocity of an unladen European swallow (bonus if you get the reference here). While useful as scheduling tools, our phones are also free for anyone you know to call, text, or message you on one of a million social apps at any time. The phone's primary function is communication and information. My theory is that because the phone can be distracting in many ways, we do not use the features that could benefit us the most—like scheduling our time.

It takes time.

Setting a schedule and following it takes time. It is an investment that you make upfront to save you time and frustration later. Let us go back to my menu example earlier in this chapter. Yes. It takes time and effort to set it up, but once it is in place, the thinking and planning are already completed. And perhaps the most significant benefit is that you will save time in the long run (or even in the short run).

In Kevin Kruse's book *15 Secrets Successful People Know About Time Management*, he states, "You can never lose time and get it back again. You can't spend time and earn more of it. You can't buy it, rent it, borrow it." Time is limited. And every second that passes is one less second you have on this planet earth. I know that sounds harsh and may be upsetting, but you need to start prioritizing your time.

A schedule will help you prioritize your time and show you what the most important tasks are. Is taking a walk with your partner important to you? Schedule it. Is playing with your kids important to you? Schedule it. Whatever it is that you value, you need to schedule it. You might be thinking, "Wow . . . I shouldn't have to schedule time with my wife or kids; I should just do it." And there is the catch. You think to yourself you should just do it, but how often does it happen?

I may have hit on my fledgling guitar desires earlier in the book. Bear with me as I want to hit on it again. I enjoy playing my guitar. I enjoy taking lessons. I like being able to play a song that I dig. So why haven't I practiced regularly (and by regularly, I mean daily)? Because it was not part of my schedule. I would have that conversation with myself that goes something like this; "I need to practice today. I want to work on that Muse song that I love. I need to get at least an hour in before my lesson on Saturday." And what happens? Nothing. I used to find myself going a week at a time without practicing. I am proud to say that I have practice time built into my schedule as of right now. I have an Amazon Echo in my office, and I have a reminder that tells me out loud, "Here is your reminder. Practice the guitar." Whatever I am doing at 9:00 am when that reminder goes off, I stop immediately and pick up my guitar.

As referenced earlier in this chapter, time is the most valuable commodity you have. More than money. More than anything. It is time that you start taking control of your time and managing it to get the most out of life.

It feels confining.

When working with clients, I often suggest scheduling time to alleviate feelings of stress and being overwhelmed with tasks. I also ask my clients to prioritize items to include time for themselves, or what I like to call self-care time. Many of my clients have expressed resistance to scheduling as they feel it would be too confining or regimented. They will sometimes state something similar to this "I don't like to be too scheduled because it feels like work." Here is the thing, my friends. All of the tasks and responsibilities are going to be there whether you schedule them or not. The advantage of scheduling is that you take control of the tasks instead of the tasks controlling you.

You might be thinking, "Okay, okay. I want to start scheduling. How do I do it?" Several different proven techniques will help you develop and follow the perfect schedule for you. You can use any of the following techniques by themselves or in combination with one another.

Proven Techniques: Four Methods
Method 1: Time Blocking

Cal Newport, the author of the book *Deep Work*, states, "A 40-hour time-blocked work week, I estimate, produces the same amount of output as a

60+ hour work week pursued without structure." Time blocking is a technique where you "block out" times in your daily schedule. Each block is dedicated to a specific task or job. Start by identifying what tasks need to be completed during your day or week. Next, estimate how much time it will take to complete each task. Plug the tasks into your calendar/schedule for the times allotted. Stick to the plan no matter what.

Here is a simple example of the time blocking method for scheduling your day:

6:00 am to 7:30 am Wake up, get ready (morning ritual)

7:30-8:00 Travel to work

8:00-8:30 Emails and social media

8:30-10:30 Work on a priority project

10:30-11:00 Return/make phone calls

11:00-12:30 pm Work on a priority project

12:30-1:00 Eat lunch

1:00-1:30 Emails and social media

1:30-3:30 Work on a priority project

3:30-4:30 Pick up kids/return home

4:30-6:00 Prep for dinner, eat, clean up

6:00-7:00 Work on a priority project or enjoyable leisure time

7:00-9:00 Free time, talk with partner, play with kids, walk the dog

9:00-9:30 Emails/social media

9:30-10:00 Evening routine/prep for bed

10:00 Read in bed

10:30 Go to sleep

This is a simple example of the time-blocking method. The important thing is to follow the schedule. While unexpected things may arise or emergencies that need to be addressed immediately, you should strictly adhere to the schedule if possible. I know there may be many who believe they are fantastic multi-taskers and that a structured schedule is not for them. A research study completed in 2010 by Jason Watson and David Stayer showed that only about 2.5% of people could multitask effectively. Suppose you are one of the 2.5%. Congratulations. For the rest of us, a structure keeps us focused and working. There is a psychological compulsion to complete a task that is scheduled.

Method 2: The Pomodoro Method

The Pomodoro method was created by a university student named Francesco Cirillo in the late 1980s.

Cirillo was struggling to complete assignments and stay focused and on-task. He told himself that he would commit to ten minutes of uninterrupted work and grabbed a tomato-shaped kitchen timer to count down the ten minutes. Pomodoro is a tomato in Italian. He found this technique to be a huge success.

Here are the steps to the Pomodoro Method:

1. Create a to-do list and set a timer.

2. Set the timer for 15, 20, or 25 minutes (don't go over 25 minutes at a time) and start working on your first task.

3. When the timer goes off, review what you have completed.

4. Take a 5-minute break.

5. Start your next "Pomodoro." After four sessions, take a 15–30-minute break

The Pomodoro Method can be viewed as "sprints" of work. Many aerobic and fitness routines use the same method to push your body physically. You perform short sprints or go "all-out" for short bursts of time with breaks in-between.

Method 3: The Most Important Task Method

Focus on just the three (or one) most vital tasks for your day and start working immediately on that task. Studies have found that we have difficulty starting with the most important and, often, the most difficult tasks because we have an aversion to working hard immediately. It is sometimes easier to get a bunch of simple items checked off of our list and work up to the "big job." By completing the most important task first, everything else becomes easier. Author James Clear states, "We often assume that productivity means getting more things done each day. Wrong. Productivity is getting important things done consistently. And no matter what you are working on, there are only a few things that are truly important." Mark Twain puts it in a bit more colorful way. "If it's your job to eat a frog, it's best to do it first thing in the morning. If it's your job to eat two frogs, it's best to eat the biggest one first."

Method 4: The Ninety Minute Focus Session

The human body works in cycles called ultradian rhythms. Ultradian rhythms are recurring cycles or periods within a twenty-four-hour day. A sleep researcher named Nathaniel Kleitman performed experiments in the 1950s and found that the human body goes through cycles during sleep. The time frame of these cycles was from ninety minutes to an hour and a half and reflected the different levels of sleep (light, REM, and deep sleep). These cycles also occur during our waking state and cause differing energy and alertness levels during the day.

The ninety-minute focus sessions take advantage of these ultradian rhythms by focusing for ninety-minute cycles. This allows you to work hard at something when your brain is at its most alert. Science has shown that after ninety minutes of brain activity, it becomes much more challenging to stay focused or be productive.

To implement the ninety-minute focus session, set a timer and work for ninety minutes straight. Once the timer goes off, immediately step away and take a twenty to thirty-minute break before returning to work. Do not do anything during the break that requires mental exertion. This approach is sometimes referred to as the "extended Pomodoro method."

Whatever approach or combination of methods you choose, implement them immediately. It may seem cumbersome and awkward when starting; however, once it becomes locked in as a habit, you will be shocked at how much wasted time is saved. Scheduling gives you control over your time and attention, and it focuses your energy to accomplish your goals. If you do not schedule things ahead of time, you will become a victim of circumstance and time, ending up doing things that are not ideal and will feel out of control. Remember, time is ticking. There are a limited number of seconds in your life. Make the most of each one.

Regardless of what method or combination of methods you choose, start now to implement these strategies. A set schedule will increase your productivity, reduce your stress level and enable you to maximize the use of your time.

Chapter 9
Failure is an Option

The year was 1970. The crew of Apollo 13 was launched into space on April 11, heading for the moon. If you have not seen the movie or read about the infamous adventure, spoilers ahead. Just two days into the mission, a routine stir of the oxygen tanks caused an explosion, crippling the service module and changing the moon landing mission into a rescue mission. The film adaptation of the mission is one of my favorites. In the film, as mission control worked on the ground to get the three astronauts home alive, flight director Gene Kranz stated, "Failure is not an option." While Kranz never actually said this, it made great drama and characterization in the movie.

But what if failure *is* an option? Can failure help you succeed? Are life lessons simply failures that we commit to not repeating? In H. Jon Benjamin's 2018 book, he states, "It's an assertion that failure is an option and even, at times, a viable prescription for a better life, despite its long-standing stigmatization.

Failure can be incredibly freeing and an end in itself, not just that tired platitude that it is a necessary step on the road to success."

We all want to succeed. We do not start projects or jobs with the intent of failing. Ask any successful person about their path in life, and they will undoubtedly tell you about failures along the way. Here are some famous successful people who failed—*a lot*.

- **Sir James Dyson**

  Well known for the invention of the famous bagless vacuums that many of us use in our homes today, Dyson had numerous challenges on his way to success. He developed 5,126 failed prototypes before creating the final product that is the standard for vacuums today.

- **Stephen Spielberg**

  Spielberg has won three Academy Awards, and his films have grossed over $9 billion. He was rejected twice by Southern California's School of Cinematic Arts.

- **Walt Disney**

  His former newspaper editor told Disney that he "lacked imagination and had no good ideas."

Failure can be disappointing and sometimes devastating, but it can also help us gain valuable skills and insights that enable us to move towards success. Did you know that a good average in baseball is .300? That means for every ten times at bat, a player makes an out seven times.

I perform hypnosis stage shows and was recently traveling to Iowa. After my flight landed in Cedar Rapids, I picked up my rental vehicle and headed out to my destination (a high school in rural Iowa). I set the GPS on my phone and started driving. However, when I arrived at my destination, I was in the middle of nowhere, on a dirt road. After closer inspection, I mistyped the address into my phone and was nowhere near where I needed to be. After making the correction and driving another thirty minutes, I arrived at my destination. The point is, I still arrived at my destination, just not with the route I intended.

Life can be the same way. We all have dreams and aspirations, and we set out on a journey to achieve these dreams. The dream may be to own your own business or become financially wealthy. There are going to be detours and failures along the way. How you manage those detours will determine whether or not you reach your final destination. You must concentrate on moving forward. Just like the stock market, it is never a straight line up or down.

So how do we manage our failures? It is essential to recognize that failure will come. It is what you do with that failure that makes a difference between those who are successful and those who are not. Unsuccessful people blame others and situations for their failures rather than dissecting what went wrong and how to correct it moving forward. Here are some practical steps to manage failure.

1. Set realistic and attainable goals.

If your goals are unrealistic and unattainable, you are setting yourself up for failure right from the start. For you musicians out there, if your expectation is that you can pick up a guitar and start playing like Eddie Van Halen in a month, your goal is not realistic. Even with realistic goals, there will be times when you fall short or make a mistake. This is part of the process of learning and growing.

2. Break up overwhelming tasks into small steps.

You may know the old saying uttered by Desmond Tutu; "There is only one way to eat an elephant; a bite at a time." The same philosophy applies to the way we approach tasks and challenges. When you are facing an immense challenge, are you overwhelmed with all that may be involved? I had this feeling when I started college. In my first semester of school, I took fifteen credit hours. A couple of months in, I remember saying to myself, "How am I ever going to get through this?" I was struggling with fifteen credits. How was I ever going to reach 120 credits for my bachelor's degree? Just like anything else, one step at a time. One assignment, one paper, one exam, and the credits just started adding up.

3. **Focus on one activity at a time.**

While many of you may consider yourselves the ultimate multi-taskers, did you know that your brain is not built to multi-task? Yes, it may feel like you are getting a lot more completed by doing five things at once. However, it is more likely you are spending a lot more time and effort than if you focused on the tasks one at a time. When you are focused on just one task, both sides of your brain are activated and work together. When you are working on multiple things at once, your brain is switching from left to right and right to left. While this switch may take a fraction of a second, those fractions add up. It will take you longer if you are multi-tasking. Also, switching sides back and forth will make your brain more prone to mistakes and drain your mental resources.

4. **Acknowledge that everyone makes mistakes.**

You are going to screw up. That is a fact. No human is infallible. The main thing I want you to focus on is how do you respond to your mistakes? If you have messed up, the best thing to do is admit it and move on. Many people have a difficult time accepting their own mistakes and feel like it reflects them as a person. I was working with a client that we will call Bob. Bob worked for a major company in the area, and he was called into his manager's office on a Friday afternoon (never a good time to visit the manager). His manager proceeded to tell Bob that he was being written up because he had been using his computer at work to conduct a side business. Bob expressed to me that he became angry and defensive and told his boss that "everyone does it." After a couple of sessions, Bob was able to admit that he made a mistake and eventually apologized to his manager for his poor response. Own your mistakes and move on.

5. Recognize failures present learning opportunities.

This fits in with the previous item. Now that you have owned your mistake, you need to learn from it. In Bob's case, he learned a valuable lesson that he should never use his work computer for personal business.

I am a huge baseball fan, and I shared some of my baseball memories earlier in the book. Let's look at two examples. First, a player goes up to bat and swings at the first pitch the pitcher throws. He hits a soft ground ball down the third baseline and reaches first base. That seems like a success, right? Second, let's look at player two. Player two goes up to bat and takes a couple of pitches—one a ball, one a strike. He fouls off a couple of pitches. He takes a couple of more pitches that were balls. Player two finally hits a sharp line drive into the outfield that is caught by a diving left fielder.

Player one got a hit. Player two made an out. Which player learned more? Player one saw only one pitch. Player two saw eight or nine pitches. He saw different types of pitches. He saw pitches that were at different speeds. He was able to pick up a pattern in the way the pitcher throws. Even though player two made an out, he gained so much more information and knowledge than the first player.

Look for learning opportunities in your failures. Figure out why you failed and what you can do differently. Author Mike Bensi states, "To be able to be successful, we have to recognize that failures are a part of the learning path."

While failure is not the ultimate goal, it is a part of any successful process or experience.

Chapter 10
Hypnosis

In this chapter, I am going to give you a brief history of hypnosis. We are then going to break it down and explain exactly what it is and how it works.

I perform comedy hypnosis stages shows as The Motor City Hypnotist, and I travel often. I have had many conversations with strangers on flights. Invariably, the question comes up "What do you do for a living?" When I state I am a hypnotist or hypnotherapist, consistently, the next question comes; "Is it real?" I'll often joke with people and say, "No, it's fake. I just fake it, and I get paid. I've made a career out of faking it." Now, of course, that is not true. Hypnosis is real, and it has been around in one form or another for thousands of years.

There are many books about hypnosis, and I could dedicate an entire book just on hypnosis itself. However, I am going to summarize as best as possible and dedicate this chapter to providing a history and covering the significant facets of hypnosis and how and why it is so effective.

The History of Hypnosis

Hypnosis has existed in some form or another for thousands of years. I do not want to bore you with a long, convoluted history lesson, but I believe it is essential to know that the roots of hypnosis go way back. It lends some credence to the effectiveness, even though early practices may have been a bit crazy.

Many ancient cultures utilized some form of hypnosis. In Egypt and Greece, they sent sick people to healing places known as sleep temples or dream temples. In ancient India, they had a book called the "Sanskrit" that described different levels of hypnosis. During the Middle Ages, people believed royalty (especially kings and princes) could heal using only a touch. This phenomenon was known as the "Royal Touch." At that time, their miraculous healings were attributed to divine power.

A Swiss physician named Paracelsus was the first to use magnets to heal people. Healing with magnets was still around into the 18th Century. During this time, a Jesuit Priest named Maximillian Hell became famous when he used magnetized steel plates and placed them on patients' bodies to heal them. One of Hell's students was an Austrian physician Franz Mesmer (a name you may recognize). The term "mesmerism" came from him. Mesmer discovered that he did not need magnets to "induce trance" and theorized that the healing force came directly from him into the patient. This was incorrect, of course. Mesmer also believed that the healing energy could come from an invisible fluid in space. See? I told you some of the old theories were pretty crazy! Incidentally, a movie is available on Netflix about Franz Mesmer and stars the late Alan Rickman. The movie title is *Mesmer*.

Some of the early pioneers of psychology studied hypnosis. Pierre Janet was a French psychologist, physician, philosopher, and psychotherapist. He lived from 1859-1947. Janet developed theories of traumatic memory and unconscious processes. Sigmund Freud also studied hypnosis and began practicing hypnosis in 1887, and even though he ditched hypnosis early on, it was crucial to his invention of psychoanalysis.

There followed an intense period of investigation of hypnosis. Several physicians developed the use of hypnosis for anesthesia. In 1834 John Elliotson, who was a British surgeon, performed many painless surgical procedures using hypnosis. James Esdaile, a Scottish surgeon, performed over 2,000 minor and 345 major operations using hypnosis in the 1840s and 1850s.

Considered the father of modern hypnosis, James Braid, an ophthalmologist, coined the term neurohypnotism. The term was later changed to hypnotism and finally became hypnosis in 1841. Braid is well known in the field of psychosomatic medicine.

Many practitioners influenced the field of hypnosis in the 20th century. Among them, American psychiatrist Milton Erickson. His theories were based on the belief that the subconscious mind is always active and listening. His approach led to further advancements in the field of hypnosis, including subliminal suggestions and neurolinguistic programming (also known as NLP).

It is interesting to note, from a historical view, although hypnosis was often attached to various passing fads and outlandish theories, the clinical practice and scientific study of hypnosis have survived. This shows that hypnosis has endured for thousands of years and continues to be used and studied today.

What Is Hypnosis?

Hypnosis, simply put, is a relaxed state of body and mind. Okay. That is as simple as it can be. Now a lot of us know how to relax our bodies. You do it when you fall asleep at night or take a nap or when you are just lying down and relaxing. Tell me if you have ever experienced this. You lie down in bed. Your body is exhausted, and you intend to go to sleep. However, your brain keeps going. It is like a runaway train. You are unable to slow it down or turn off your thinking. You may be thinking about money issues, or a conflict you have had with your spouse, or any other hundreds of thoughts and worries.

When I started my clinic many years ago, I spent many hours ruminating with worry and stress. For any of you who are business owners or entrepreneurs, you can probably relate to this. I had to concentrate and focus my mind on using hypnotic techniques to shut off the noise in my head. Sometimes it is more challenging.

Hypnosis quiets your brain and relaxes your thinking. That is the foundation of how hypnosis works. With hypnosis, you relax your body and your mind. Imagine your mind has two compartments. I know this is not physiologically correct. But imagine there are two compartments. The front compartment is your conscious mind. Your conscious mind is what you use to talk, interact, and evaluate what is happening. You use your conscious mind when you are reading or watching television, or having a conversation with someone. You are engaging in an activity, and you are using your conscious mind to evaluate, learn and formulate responses. The back compartment is your subconscious mind. The subconscious mind controls involuntary actions like breathing and bodily functions. It is automatic. The subconscious mind is also where all your habits are stored, whether good or bad.

Hypnosis is often described as a "trance-like-state." While that is true, the perception of trance is often misunderstood. If you observe someone who is in a hypnotic trance, it appears they are in a sleep-like state and "out of it." In fact, the opposite is true. Even though it looks like sleep, the subject is in a state of focused attention, heightened suggestibility, and vivid fantasies. If you are in a state of hypnosis, you are hyper-aware. It is much easier to make changes to your thinking in this state, which ultimately leads to change in behaviors and feelings.

The Process of Hypnosis

The process of hypnosis is straightforward. It starts before you even arrive at your hypnotherapist's office or show. Just thinking about hypnosis has already begun the process. The pre-talk (or introduction) is the most vital stage of a successful hypnosis session. When I see a first-time client, I start by asking them, "what do you know about hypnosis?" Responses vary, but typically, clients will tell me about a movie or TV show depicting hypnosis. I have never seen hypnosis portrayed accurately in Hollywood movies or TV shows. Most of the representations do a disservice to the field of hypnosis. They often portray mind control or somehow being stuck in hypnosis. We will address more myths and misconceptions later in this chapter.

I share with the client that hypnosis is a naturally occurring state that we all experience daily. Any activity that requires your complete and focused attention and blocks out all other stimuli is a state of hypnosis. If you are engrossed in a movie or book, and everything else is blocked out, you are in a state of hypnosis. There is a term used in sports aptly named "being in the zone." When an athlete is "in the zone," things appear to be happening automatically without conscious thought. Athletes will often state something to the effect of "it was all just happening, and I wasn't even thinking about it." Once you know that hypnosis is a naturally occurring state and that you experience it regularly, your conscious mind becomes more open and accepting of the process.

The next step is beginning the relaxation process. In hypnosis language, this part is called induction. It involves talking you through the steps of relaxing your body and your mind. This can be done in any number of ways. Often, relaxing music can be played while the hypnotist directs you to breathe deeply, focusing on relaxing your muscles. I always use terms such as imagine and feel. I might say, "imagine your eyelids are so heavy that it is becoming difficult to keep them open" or "notice how your hands feel right now as they become light or heavy." Once your body and mind are in a deep, relaxed state, we move on to the suggestion stage.

As described earlier, once your mind is relaxed, I start speaking to the subconscious part of your mind. For example, if a client has come to see me to stop smoking, I will provide suggestions such as "smoking is simply something you used to do." This frames the habit as something from your past and not something current. I also focus on eliminating connections or triggers for smoking such as coffee, alcohol, driving, or any other situations that may have triggered smoking.

Next, I encourage you to imagine yourself going throughout your day smoke-free. How would you feel? What would be different in your life? Future framing is a crucial component of hypnosis and allows you to see yourself with the changes implemented.

Finally, I typically ask you to visualize a color. This is what hypnotists refer to as a mental anchor. Anchoring is something you already experience and is attached to senses (sight, taste, touch, smell). When you smell freshly baked cookies, does it remind you of mom? When you hear a specific song, does it remind you of a person or place from your past? This is an example of anchoring and how it makes permanent connections between your senses and feelings. I then direct you to press your thumb and forefinger together to create a physical anchor. These anchors allow you to be aware and trigger associated suggestions and reactions "planted" during the hypnosis session.

A hypnosis session ends with the hypnotist typically counting up and bringing you out of trance and back to full alertness with the suggestions now fully embedded into your subconscious thinking.

As stated before, I could write a whole book on the process and techniques of hypnosis. This is just a brief, high-level overview of the structure of a hypnosis session that will give you insight and familiarity with the process itself.

Can I Be Hypnotized?

This is the question I get most often when I am traveling or speaking to strangers about hypnosis. There is conflicting information online referencing the effectiveness of hypnosis. Much of this information is anecdotal. One story suggests that only 80% of people can be hypnotized. I believe that everyone can be hypnotized given the right environment, process, and timeframe. Some of my clients can be hypnotized instantly, while others may take a session or two to let go of their critical faculties.

It is important to note that people who have focus issues such as ADD/ADHD will have a more difficult time with hypnosis as it does require you to follow directions and intense focus on the clinician's directions. If you fear giving up control, you may have more difficulty entering the hypnotic state. Individuals who are very analytical and skeptical may also have a more challenging time. An essential part of the hypnotic process is a relationship of trust between the subject and the hypnotist.

As referenced earlier in this chapter, we all experience some form of hypnosis daily. In most cases, you may be unaware of these states, reinforcing the idea that you are not overthinking or being too analytical.

Long answer short, everyone can be hypnotized. The path to get there is often different and unique for everyone. The only reason you would be unable to be hypnotized is something within yourself not allowing it to happen.

Misconceptions

Many people are resistant or skeptical about hypnosis. This is caused primarily because of the misconceptions and false beliefs that individuals may have. As mentioned earlier, I have never seen hypnosis portrayed accurately in movies or TV. These inaccurate portrayals have reinforced false ideas and theories about hypnosis which I hope to dispel here.

- **Hypnosis is mind control.**

  This is one of the most common misconceptions I hear when speaking with clients or performing shows. Of course, this is based on the longstanding characterizations of hypnotists as sorcerers or magicians. I can guarantee you that I have no powers of sorcery, although I do know a few magic tricks. Mind control is a coercive process. It involves getting someone to think or do something against their will and impairs their ability to think independently. Hypnosis is a collaborative process between the hypnotist and the volunteer. You will never do anything against your will while hypnotized. I use this example when I am performing stage shows. If I hypnotized Bob and told him that he would get up and punch the first person he sees in the face when I snap my fingers, of course, Bob would not do that (unless that is something Bob would normally do). First, I would never give anyone that type of suggestion, and second, you would reject any suggestion outside of your moral and ethical beliefs.

- **You can get stuck in a trance.**

The unequivocal answer is no. As stated earlier, hypnosis is a natural state that we all enter in and out of regularly. This fear goes back to my comments on the media portrayal of hypnosis and false beliefs.

There was a recent hypnosis incident that I would like to address here. I won't provide the specific names or organizations; however, I believe it is important to learn from this. Long story short, a hypnotist was recently performing a stage show at a college orientation event. During the show, many of the students were "stuck" in a trance. Some of the students became emotional. Many were crying and having panic attacks. The news coverage of this event portrayed the idea that these students were indeed "stuck."

Without being critical of either the hypnotist or the students, here is my take on this. Disclaimer: I was not at this show and am providing my opinion. First, the students were under the assumption that they could be stuck. This idea must be debunked before a show even begins. Second, hypnosis will sometimes bring about an emotional response. Many of my clients have never been as relaxed as they are during hypnosis. Therefore, an emotional response is not unusual. Third, an emotional reaction from one person is likely to influence another person. Once the emotional responses started spreading, it undoubtedly scared other students, and panic ensued. Fourth, there is a phenomenon, especially with high school and college-aged students, for attention-seeking, especially after a show.

I have performed hundreds of shows all over the United States, and a handful of times, I have had volunteers approach me after a show stating they were stuck in a trance. I informed them that it is not possible, as addressed in my pre-talk. These volunteers have been in such a relaxed state for an hour or hour and a half that they feel different. They are experiencing a feeling they are not used to, and therefore, the belief is that they are stuck.

Finally, hypnosis feels so good that many people do not want to come out. They are resistant to letting go of that relaxed feeling. Ultimately, it is your choice, and you are entirely in control.

- **You will tell secrets when hypnotized.**

Another myth debunked. As emphasized previously, you are in total control when experiencing hypnosis. You will not do or say anything you do not want to. You will only reveal information you are comfortable and willing to reveal. In my practice, I often work with clients to explore past events and experiences to understand behaviors. The client will still only provide the information they are comfortable providing.

- **Hypnosis doesn't work.**

This is one of the most common myths about hypnosis. I have been practicing clinically for almost thirty years. I have worked with countless clients to address smoking cessation, weight loss, anxiety reduction, sports performance enhancement, and many other issues. I can tell you from experience that hypnosis is an effective tool for change. History has shown many respected psychoanalysts and hypnotherapists who have documented amazing results, and hypnosis is recognized by the American Medical Association, British Medical Association, American Psychological Association, and British Psychological Association (along with many other organizations).

So now, how can we use hypnosis to guarantee your success? In the next and last chapter, we will walk through a hypnosis session to implement all the strategies developed throughout this book.

Chapter 11
Empower Your Mind

This is the chapter where we put it all together. The purpose of this book is to guide you to a different result. Chapter 1 was This Time It Will Be Different. That is my goal for you, my friend. This time it will be different. We defined your why. What is it that drives you and gives you purpose? This is your why. I explained how to guarantee failure and covered all of the things you have now decided that you will leave behind. We addressed beliefs and how they affect your behaviors and results, and how to remove limiting beliefs from your life along with procrastination. Practical things such as motivation and scheduling will be your new regular. Remember how we talked about the value of time. I appreciate that you have invested your precious time to read this book, and now I want you to implement what you have read.

We are going to start by walking you through a hypnosis session. During this session, you will focus on the changes you have made and embed this new, better way of thinking into your subconscious mind. This will lead to massive success.

I know it may seem a bit weird to read through a hypnosis session. However, if you follow my instructions and practice, this will become second nature to you. Let me emphasize that hypnosis does not feel like anything. It is simply feeling relaxed. There is no lightning bolt or spell that will zap you into a hypnotic trance. If your mind and body are relaxed, you are in a state of trance.

First, find a comfortable place where you will not be disturbed or distracted. Start with deep breaths in through your nose and out through your mouth. Make them very deep breaths, all the way down to your diaphragm. Continue to breathe deeply in through your nose and out through your mouth. I want you to focus on the sensations in your body as you continue to breathe deeply in . . . and slowly out. Your hands and feet may start to feel tingly, or heavy, or light. Whatever that feeling is to you, focus on the change. Focus on the feeling as you continue to breathe deeply in and slowly out. And as you sit or lie there, you might have noticed you have already started to feel a change.

Do not worry if your relaxation pulls you away from these words or this book. You can come right back and continue reading. Just do what feels good for you.

Begin tightening and releasing your muscles, starting at the top of your head and working your way down your body—head, face, neck, shoulders, back, arms, hands, stomach, midsection, thighs, calves, feet, toes. Tighten and relax each area one by one. Take your time. Hold for a couple of seconds and release, then move on to the next group of muscles. Once you have completed all the muscle groups, notice the change. Notice the feeling of complete physical relaxation. A person may not know . . . you have all the resources you need to continue to relax even further.

Focus now on how you feel. It is much different than it was a few moments ago, is it not? Continue to imagine yourself floating, drifting, sinking, deeper and deeper into relaxation. Imagine yourself now, standing at the top of a staircase or possibly in an elevator. Count down slowly in your mind from 10.....9.......8......7......6......5......4......3......2 ......1. Just letting go, letting it happen, sinking further and further into that wonderful world of relaxation.

Take a few moments now to notice how different you feel. It is even more different than it was just a couple of moments ago, right? Focus on the sensation of relaxation, the feeling of being totally and completely relaxed.

At this point, you are going to say to yourself the following suggestions. You can say them out loud or in your mind.

From this moment going forward, it will be different. It will be more different than it has ever been. I have already decided to change, and I'm just locking it in, confirming it in my subconscious mind.

I genuinely believe that this time is going to be different. I will experience different results than I ever have before.

I will feel more confident than I ever have before.

I know what my why is.

Tell yourself now precisely what your why is. Focus on what you are passionate about. Think about what brings you happiness and joy. Imagine yourself right now feeling a sense of purpose and motivation because you love what you do. Whatever that thing is, think about it right now and commit to making it happen. Imagine yourself a week from now... . . a month from now . . . a year from now, doing what you love to do, and experience success you may have only dreamed about in the past.

Imagine your life as you eliminate habits and things that have held you back in the past. You take ownership of all of your actions. You are committed to your health and wellness, including taking care of yourself physically, mentally, emotionally, and spiritually. You will do things differently from now on. You will change your habits, your schedule, your interactions with others. You will let go of anger and frustration and focus on peace and serenity. You will challenge yourself with new experiences. You will commit to long-term success and know that you will have the effort, tenacity, and motivation to make it happen. You will not give up when you meet challenges but will be excited at the opportunity to meet those challenges and become better because of them. You will begin using your free time to learn, connect, and advance your life and dreams. You will start doing things that you have only talked about in the past and be excited about the challenge. You will meet and find new people who support you and your future vision and use that support to propel you to new heights. You will ask for help when you need it and know that it is not weakness but strength. You will never quit or give up because you know the results are worth it.

From this point going forward, you are aware that you can only control two things: your thoughts and your actions. Anything else does not matter. All of your energy is now committed to your thoughts and your actions. Your beliefs are now different than they ever have been before. Imagine being free of past feelings of doubt and insecurity. Imagine being totally and utterly confident as you only focus on your thoughts and feelings.

See yourself moving forward with all past limiting beliefs erased from your mind. You are committed to using the techniques to identify and remove those limiting beliefs. Play a new movie of yourself in your mind right now. How are you different. What has changed? Focus on the new and positive changes that will transform your thinking and your life.

Gone is procrastination. You will be decisive and take action every day. You will not avoid or put off tasks. Your motivation is now at an all-time high. You will wake up each day motivated to act and move your progress forward.

You will sleep between seven and eight hours every night and feel great physically and mentally.

You will learn from failures and be excited about the knowledge they provide. You are confident that there is valuable information and lessons to be learned in every situation that will only make you better and stronger.

You now feel compelled to implement scheduling strategies that will ensure you maximize your productivity and save valuable time.

I want you to imagine yourself a year from now. What will you look like? What will you feel like? How will you be different than you are today?

Take a couple of deep breaths in and out. Focus on the feeling of relaxation and re-orient yourself to the room you are in. Notice right now how different you think and feel.

It may have been challenging for you to read while trying to implement the process laid out in the previous pages. That is why I have made a full recording just for you. If you would like to receive the hypnosis above in audio format for your own private listening pleasure, please visit

https://detroithypnotist.convertri.com/empower-your-mind-for-success-mp3 to download an audio file.

~ ~ ~

It is my hope that having read this book, you have changed your life and your future. Let me know about your success! www.motorcityhypnotist.com

You can also visit me at www.motorcityhypnotist.com for more information, products and details regarding show and appearance bookings. Please also join me on the Motor City Hypnotist Podcast which is available on all podcast platforms.

Please also join my private Facebook group Empower Your Mind for Success at

https://www.facebook.com/groups/345625973445594

Change Your Thinking, Change Your Life!

Made in the USA
Monee, IL
04 September 2021